CLASSICAL MUSIC OF INDIA

Dr L. Subramaniam, India's violin icon and the creator of the Global Fusion concept, has variously been called 'the Paganini of Indian classical music', 'the God of the Indian violin' and 'Violin Chakravarthy'. In a career spanning over six decades, he has produced, performed, conducted or collaborated on close to two hundred recordings.

Subramaniam is the only musician who has performed/ recorded Carnatic classical music, Western classical music, composed for and conducted major orchestras, scored for films and collaborated with some of the greatest musicians from different genres of music, including jazz, Western classical, jugalbandis (with north Indian musicians), world music and global fusion. He has established himself as a force that is strongly Indian, but universal in nature and approach.

He is the founder-director of the Lakshminarayana Global Music Festival, the biggest global music festival in India, as also of the Subramaniam Academy of Performing Arts (SaPa), a premier institute for musical education, and the Lakshminarayana Global Centre of Excellence (LGCE).

He has received several awards and honours, including the Padma Bhushan and the Sangeet Natak Akademi Award for 'The Most Creative Artist', and holds a PhD in music.

Viji Subramaniam, also known as Vijayashree Subramaniam (1952–95) was a singer, composer, author and multilinguist.

As a vocalist, she won a number of prestigious awards, including the All India Radio 'President of India' medal in 1972. She also received a Master's degree in music from the California Institute of the Arts.

After marrying violinist L. Subramaniam in 1976, she collaborated with him on many of his projects, including his early fusion albums. She also sang for the soundtracks of two acclaimed films by the Indian director Mira Nair: *Salaam Bombay!* (1988; winner of both the Cannes Film Festival Audience Award and the Academy Award for Best Foreign Language Film) and *Mississippi Masala* (1991).

In 1992, Viji and L. Subramaniam launched the Lakshminarayana Global Music Festival (LGMF) in the memory of Professor V. Lakshminarayana, her father-in-law.

She died in February 1995 after a long battle with cancer.

L. SUBRAMANIAM
AND VIJI SUBRAMANIAM

CLASSICAL MUSIC OF INDIA

A PRACTICAL GUIDE

First published by Tranquebar, an imprint of Westland Publications Private Limited, in 2018

This revised edition published by Westland Non-Fiction, an imprint of Westland Books, a division of Nasadiya Technologies Private Limited, in 2025

No. 269/2B, First Floor, 'Irai Arul', Vimalraj Street, Nethaji Nagar, Alapakkam Main Road, Maduravoyal, Chennai 600095

ISBN: 9789360457549

10 9 8 7 6 5 4 3 2

Typeset by Jojy Philip, New Delhi

Printed at Manipal Technologies Limited, Manipal

Contents

Prologue 1

1. A Brief History of Indian Music 4
2. The Elements of Music 33
3. The Notation System 38
4. Introduction to the Melodic Systems of Indian Classical Music 57
5. Rhythmic Concepts 96
6. Comparison between Carnatic (South Indian) and Hindustani (North Indian) Music 124
7. Musical Instruments 153
8. Musical Forms 183

Appendix 202

Epilogue 214

Prologue

I began my musical journey at a very young age, learning from my father and guru, Professor V. Lakshminarayana. My father gave me a solid foundation in both the theory and practice of Carnatic music. Apart from being a great violinist and singer, he was also extremely knowledgeable in music theory. It was his teaching and vision that later helped me learn other genres of music and subsequently adapt those idioms into my Global Fusion concept, which I started in the 1970s.

After I completed my Bachelor's degree in medicine, I wanted to switch over to music and sought admission into the California Institute of the Arts. I was so homesick that I completed the MFA (Master of Fine Arts) course in nine months, but the university said that they couldn't award me the degree before I had completed two years in the campus. So, they offered me a teaching position. I had to teach students from different musical backgrounds, and some of them had absolutely no exposure to Indian music. At that point, we didn't have too many books on Indian music; those that were written weren't easily accessible; and even those that were accessible emphasised the historical and mythological aspects of our music. In my view, there was a need for a book that could be a handy guide of music theory, which could be of use to a practical musician and an aspiring composer. To my knowledge, such a book did not exist, and therefore, I began writing down a few things based on my father's handwritten notes and the research that I conducted with my late wife, Viji Subramaniam. She worked with me extensively on this and we published the book *Euphony* in the 1990s.

The present book has been further developed, trying to reach people at all levels of musical interest: from the common reader and music enthusiast to practical musicians, composers and musicologists. It starts off with a brief historical overview of Indian music, mostly to acquaint the reader with the evolution of musical thought in India over the past five thousand years. Before going into the basics of melody and rhythm, it is useful to get a working knowledge of the notation system (which is quite straightforward). The concepts of melody and rhythm in Carnatic music are highly developed, and anyone who understands these in practice will have equipped himself or herself with some of the most powerful tools available in the music toolbox. We then take a look at the various musical forms in Carnatic music and Hindustani music, including the dhrupad genre. The fifth chapter gives an idea of the richness and variety of musical instruments used in India.

A sound knowledge of Indian classical music will benefit musicians and composers everywhere; it will broaden their horizons and give ample scope for greater creativity. The scientifically structured concept of melakarta ragas (parent scales) and nadais (dividing a beat into multiple pulses) will create many possibilities for musicians to explore the melodic and rhythmic aspects of their own music in a new light. I'm currently working on my next book *Raga Harmony*, which is basically an adaptation of the thesis that I presented for my PhD. Starting out with a new formulation of thirty-six parent scales that encompasses all possible melodic scales, I have set out to explain the concept of 'raga harmony', which I created while I was in the US, working on new ideas to blend the music of the East and the West, especially to create orchestral compositions.

While writing this book, I have heavily drawn from the research that my late wife Viji Subramaniam had done while we co-wrote

Euphony. The present work would not be possible but for all the material that I have taken from the earlier book. In the preparation of this, I have been assisted by my daughter, Bindu as well as my disciple Hari Ravikumar. In the preparation of the sections related to Hindustani music, I have been greatly helped by Sukanya Purkayastha, Chaya Ganguli and Tanmoy Bose. Vivaswath Rao assisted me in the re-working of a few chapters. Without all their help, I wouldn't have been able to bring out this book in time. Special thanks to my wife, Kavita, for being an insipration. My sons, Naryana and Ambi, my granddaughter, Mahati and the rest of my family have always supported me in all my activities. My sincere thanks to all of them.

Dr L. Subramaniam
November 2024

1

A Brief History of Indian Music

It is not possible to run through the entire history of Indian music in one chapter because of the complexities and the length of time over which it has developed, from the Vedic period to the present. This is merely an overview of the historical development of Indian classical music, starting from the Vedas, which are more than five thousand years old, to the present time.

Indian classical music is one of the most complex systems of music in the world, with a highly developed melodic and rhythmic structure. It does not owe its origins to folk music although it may have at some point been influenced by it.

Music was traditionally given the first and foremost position in the sixty-four arts of ancient India. In addition to being deeply involved with spirituality, rituals and important life events in Indian society, music also developed as an independent art form, which has been performed on stage outside of the religious context for centuries.

Archaeological excavations made in the early 1920s in India made us aware of the existence of the Sindhu–Saraswati civilisation (earlier known as the Indus Valley civilisation). According to recent research, this civilisation dates back to around 6000 BCE. Some prominent historians believe that the Sindhu–Saraṣwati civilisation formed the basis of the Vedic culture that came later. The 'Vedic' in Vedic culture comes from 'Veda', the ancient sacred literature of the Hindus. Hindus are those who practise Hinduism, arguably the oldest religion in the world. Many consider it more a way of life than a religion. The word 'veda' means 'knowledge' in Sanskrit and is derived from the Sanskrit word 'vid' which means 'to know'.

There is evidence to indicate that several practices of modern Hinduism can be traced back to the Indus Valley civilisation. It is a generally accepted fact that the Vedas are the source of Indian music, which has developed over the centuries into the sophisticated system it is today.

Indian history is so steeped in mythology that, at times, it is difficult to tell where one ends and the other begins. Hindus believe that all learning and art come from a divine source. The three great deities in Hinduism are Brahma the creator, Vishnu the preserver and Shiva the destroyer of the universe. One school of thought credits Brahma for the creation of the Vedas and of music, since music had its origin in *Sama* Veda (one of the four Vedas).

Saraswati, the consort of Brahma, depicted in sculptures and paintings as holding a veena and a book, is worshipped as the goddess of fine arts and learning. Even today in south India, a particular day of the year is set aside for celebration when all instruments and books are placed before vigrahas (idols) or paintings of Saraswati and special prayers are offered to her seeking her blessings. The Saraswati Puja is similarly celebrated in north India as well.

In Hindu philosophy, music is considered a way to attain salvation, and there is a strong connection between music and the divine. Many of the south Indian music composers were actually saint-poets, whose compositions were spontaneous offerings to the Supreme, that were created in a temple or prayer setting (as opposed to a performance setting). Classical Indian music was traditionally passed down in the oral tradition.

The history of Indian music can be divided into four periods:

1. The Ancient period (from prehistoric times to 400 CE)

2. The Medieval period (from the fifth century to the fifteenth century)
3. The Modern period (from the sixteenth century to the mid-twentieth century)
4. The Post-Independence period (from the mid-twentieth century onwards)

In general, the development of Indian music can be traced through important milestones: literature, treatises on music, inscriptions and the work of musicologists and composers who have shaped, systematised and moulded Indian music into what it is today.

THE ANCIENT PERIOD

Vedas

As mentioned earlier, Indian music had its origin in the Vedas. They are also known as shruti or revealed divine truth. Four in number, the Vedas contain thousands of sukthas (hymns) in Sanskrit. These hymns were used to preserve a body of poetry, invocations and mythology in the form of chants dedicated to deities. They were passed down by oral tradition from generation to generation and were written down only much later. Both the texts and the rituals remain unchanged to this day. The four Vedas are:

1. *Rig* Veda
2. *Yajur* Veda
3. *Sama* Veda
4. *Atharva* Veda

The earliest hymns of the *Rig* Veda seem to have been composed more than six thousand years ago.[1] The *Rig* Veda was at first recited in a monotone known as archika gana. This was later developed into

[1] Shrikant G. Talageri, *The Rigveda and the Avesta: The Final Evidence*, Aditya Prakashan, 2008; David Frawley, *Gods, Sages & Kings: Vedic Secrets of Ancient Civilization*, Lotus Press, 1991.

a two-toned chant, the gathika, to be subsequently replaced by a three-toned chant, or the samika. In the samika, there was one main tone (swarita) and two accents, one higher (udatta) and one lower (anudatta). The accents were based on the requirement to emphasise certain portions of the text.

The *Yajur* Veda, which consists mainly of ritualistic descriptions, mentions the veena, as an accompaniment to vocal recitations during yajnas (Vedic fire rituals). By this time, the chants had evolved to two main tones and two accents forming a tetrachord (first four notes).

The *Sama* Veda laid the foundation for Indian music. It added three more tones to the existing tetrachord, resulting in the first full scale of seven notes. Within this scale were all the important and known musical intervals (the distances between two notes). The concept of the octave was also mentioned here.

The *Atharva* Veda is a collection of hymns composed by Sage Atharvan.

In the Vedic age, the hymns were chanted with different notes while performing yajnas and other rites. The earliest reference to musical theory is found in the *Rik Pratisakhya*, which mentions the three tones from which we get the notes of the saptaka (octave). The *Rik Pratisakhya* is the grammar of the *Rig* Veda and one of six treatises which belong to the same period as the Upanishads.

Upanishads

The Upanishads are the concluding portions of the Vedas and contain their essence. They are considered a class of literature independent of the Vedic hymns. They are the highest and purest expression of speculative thought in India and are the foundation on which most of the later philosophies and religions of India are based.

It is in the Upanishads (c. 2000 BCE) that the Indian solfège system of seven notes is discussed, as opposed to the Western solfège system that was developed by the Italian Benedictine monk, Guido D'Arezzo (990–1050 CE). There is also mention of adhara shadja, or keeping the tonic (Sa) constant, so that all melodies could be sung with this note as the base.

THE EPICS

The two great epics of India are the Ramayana and the Mahabharata. The epics deal with intellectual behaviour and the duties and obligations of man towards his peers, his family and society. They have universal appeal since human nature is the same everywhere. The Mahabharata contains the Bhagavad Gita (the Divine Song) which contains the essence of the Upanishads. The Gita is the advice given by Krishna to his friend Arjuna on the battlefield of Kurukshetra. It is a work of Hindu philosophy that has had the greatest influence on the minds of Hindus.

In the Ramayana and the Mahabharata, one can find references to grama ragas (possibly an early form of the raga concept). In the Ramayana, the poet Valmiki talks of Lava and Kusa (sons of Rama) singing in his court, and it also refers to jatis (system of modes) and murcchanas (heptatonic scales), as also to instruments like the veena.

In music, theory generally follows practice. It is difficult to imagine a theoretical concept being developed before the practical application in any art form. For example, while developing the seventy-two melakarta (parent scales) system, Venkatamakhi, the eminent musician and musicologist, based his classification of parent and derived scales on certain ragas that were practised and commonly used.

Dattilam

Dattilam (c. fourth century to first century BCE) is an ancient Indian musical text ascribed to the sage Dattila, which is alluded to in the *Natyashastra*. Written in two hundred and forty-four verses, *Dattilam* marks the transition from sama-gana or ritual *Sama* Vedic chants, to gandharva-gana, or music as an independent art form. *Dattilam* expounds concepts of swara (note), sthana (position), murcchana, alankara (embellishment, elaboration), tana (combination of note sequences) and grama (groups of notes), which contain twenty-two microtones or shrutis in an octave. The melodic structure consists of eighteen groups called jati, and it predates the raga system.

Natyashastra

The oldest record of Indian drama, dance and music theory can be found in the treatise *Natyashastra* (the science of drama) attributed to Bharata (first century BCE). This text on dramaturgy deals with music only as part of the dramatic spectacle. Yet, it is an authoritative source for musicology. This work talks about twenty-two shrutis in an octave, murcchanas, jatis, gramas (groups of notes) and the shadava (hexatonic) and audava (pentatonic) scales. There are also chapters on musical instruments which classify them into tata vadya (stringed instruments), avanaddha vadya (instruments covered with stretched membrane or skin), ghana vadya (solid instruments) and susira vadya (hollowed-out instruments). This is very similar to a classification published in the West in the early 1900s.

Brihaddesi

Brihaddesi is another important work on music. It was written by the muni Matanga in Sanskrit (fifth century CE). Besides covering topics like gramas and jatis that the *Natyashastra* also mentions, Matanga also talks about ragas, which had taken the place of jatis, and states that ragas are known as jatis because they were born of microtones (shrutis), initial notes (grahas) and clusters of tones. Also, as the realisation of aesthetic sentiments is possible from them, they are known as jatis.

The works of Matanga (*Brihaddesi*), Narada (*Sangita Makaranda,* twelfth century CE) and others of that time all throw light on the gradual development of the art of music, which was slowly breaking away from drama and dance, although there were no spectacular changes until much later. The most notable development was that of jatis being recognised as full-fledged ragas having distinctive colours and styles of singing. The contributions of Matanga and Narada are similar to that of Bharata, describing the growth of the raga system, the technique of singing with graces and embellishments, and classifying them according to the times of day when they could be sung. The *Sangita Makaranda* is the first to classify feminine and neutral ragas. Later on, they were classified into male (raga), female (ragini) and their progeny (putra).

TAMIL MUSIC

It appears that music developed independently in the Tamil region. The nomenclature used in Tamil music is different from that of the Sanskrit treatises, but the theory seems to be similar to that found in Bharata's *Natyashastra*. The *Silappadikaram*, written in Tamil by Ilango Adigal (fifth century CE), contains some of the earliest expositions of the musical scale. The seven notes were called kural, tuttam, kaikkilai, ulai, ili, vilari and taram and the microtones were called alagus. The parent scales were called panns and the derived scales were called tirims.

The Tevaram trinity (seventh century CE) are among the early Tamil composers of the sacred hymns known as the Tevarams. Tevarams were typically composed in panns (scales) and passed down orally from one generation to the other. Appar was one of the three Shaivite (followers of Shiva) saints known as the muvar (literally, three people). The other two were Tirujnana Sambandar and Sundarar.

Appar is also known as Tirunavukkarasar. He was born a Hindu but converted to Jainism. He soon became a Jain leader and was called Dharmasena. Later, however, he returned to Hinduism. He is credited with having composed about forty thousand verses but not even a tenth of these have survived.

It is believed that Tirujnana Sambandar was the youngest composer ever. He is said to have composed his first song when he was still a toddler. He lived only for sixteen years but within his short life he is believed to have written sixteen thousand verses. Less than four thousand have survived. Sambandar toured around the country singing his songs in praise of Shiva, accompanied by a yazh (an ancient string instrument) player.

Sundarar or Sundaramurti, the third of the Tevaram muvar, also lived a short life. He died at the young age of eighteen but not before he made a great contribution to the Tevarams.

The most important composer of the Tevarams was Manikkiyavasagar (tenth century CE). He was born in Vadavur in the Thanjavur district in Tamil Nadu.

Manikkiyavasagar was the composer of the *Tiruvasagam*, which consists of seven hundred songs, comprising three of his works, *Tiruvembavai*, *Kuyirpattu* and *Tirupalliyezhuchi*. A Brahmin by birth, he was a great devotee of Shiva. His forefathers were ministers in the court of the Pandya kings who ruled Tamil Nadu at that time. He was also a minister in the court of the Pandyan king. His name at birth was Vadavurar since he was born in Vadavur. Due to the superior quality of his work, he was given the name of Manikkiyavasagar which means 'one whose words are like gems'.

His compositions would, at first, be recited but due to their perfect metre, they lent themselves very well to music too. They were sung in Mohanam (a pentatonic scale), an ancient raga. His work which contains philosophical ideas, written with great simplicity, is highly revered.

Arunagirinathar (fifteenth century) was a great saint-poet and the creator of the Tiruppugazh form. Meaning 'Praise of the Lord', Tiruppugazh are devotional songs in Tamil. Arunagirinathar was a master of Tamil and Sanskrit. His compositions are known for the rare, unusual time-signatures he used, many of which do not have any names. He was given the title of Chhandapavalapperuman, meaning unequalled master of the verse. He wrote many songs in the thirty-five talas, hundred and seventy-five talas as well as the hundred and eight talas (see the chapter Rhythmic Concepts for more information about talas). He was a prolific composer and is believed to have composed sixteen thousand songs, of which there are only about two thousand left. He used the mudra (signature word) Perumal in his Tiruppugazh.

He travelled to many temples, singing songs in praise of various deities. His work *Bhuta Vetala Vaguppu* contains information about some ragas, panns, the hundred and eight talas and some percussion instruments, making it valuable from a historical point of view.

Three other prominent composers in the Tamil music tradition are Muthuthandavar, Marimutha Pillai and Arunachala Kavi. Muthuthandavar (1560–1640) from Seerkazhi composed kritis in Tamil primarily on Lord Shiva of Chidambaram. He composed sixty kirtanais (kritis) and twenty-five padams (See the chapter Musical Forms to learn about kritis and padams). Muthuthandavar is one of the earliest composers of the kriti form. Marimutha Pillai (1712–87) was born in Thillaividangam, near Chidambaram. He is said to have composed fifty kritis and padams of which twenty-five are available. His compositions are also in praise of Lord Shiva of Chidambaram. Arunachala Kavirayar (1711–79) was born in Thillaiyadi, close to Seerkazhi. He was well-versed in Tamil, Sanskrit and Telugu. His most popular work is the *Ramanatakam,* the first musical drama in Tamil. Kavirayar wrote the lyrics and the music was composed by two of his disciples, Kodandarama Iyer and Venkatarama Iyer. Some scholars refer to these three composers as the 'Adi mummurtigal', the first musical trinity of Carnatic music.

THE MEDIEVAL PERIOD

Gita Govinda

A monumental work of the medieval period is the *Gita Govinda* written in the twelfth century by the great Sanskrit poet, Jayadeva. He was born in the village of Kenduli, close to the city of Puri, famous for the Jagannath Temple, in what is modern-day Odisha. This work was the first to set melody and rhythm together in a uniform pattern. This is known as chhanda prabandha (chhanda means 'metre' and prabandha means 'composition'). In earlier compositions in Tamil, music like the Tevarams, there is mention only of the panns (ragas) in which they were composed. In *Tiruppugazh,* only the rhythmic patterns (talas) are mentioned. In *Gita Govinda,* Jayadeva gives the raga and tala for each of the songs, though the original tunes are no longer available to us. They are the earliest examples of regular musical compositions, each song (Gita) having a particular raga and tala, the tala being determined by the metre of each Sanskrit verse.

The work is divided into twelve chapters called sargas and each chapter consists of twenty-four songs. Each song, called ashtapadi, has eight sections (ashta meaning eight, padas meaning lines). *Gita Govinda* has both religious and musical significance—the songs are known for their beautiful metres and inspiring texts in praise of Radha and Krishna. It deals with the love and devotion of Radha towards Krishna. Jayadeva adopts the nayaka-nayaki format which was much used in those days. The three characters are Krishna, who is the nayaka (hero), Radha, the nayaki (heroine) and the sakhi (friend) who helps and advises Radha through her separation from Krishna and her sufferings, and ultimately unites the two lovers. On a higher level, the nayaki is the devotee, the nayaka the Lord and the sakhi the teacher or jnana guru (jnana meaning knowledge and guru meaning teacher) who guides the devotee on the right path to attain salvation (mukti).

Jayadeva was a great devotee of Krishna and he sang the ashtapadis in the temple where his wife, Padmavati, danced to them. These songs are still sung today in temples and also in concerts. They are an integral part of Odissi, the classical dance form of Odisha, Jayadeva's birthplace. Though the melodies have changed, the poetry and the metre have remained the same. The ashtapadis are sung all over India since they were written before Indian music got split into two systems—Hindustani and Carnatic music.

Sangita Ratnakara

Another important musical treatise, the *Sangita Ratnakara,* was written by Sarangadeva (1210–47). Sarangadeva was a native of Kashmir who migrated to the south and worked for the Yadava king, Raja Sodhala, in Devagiri, now in Maharashtra. In this work, he classified ragas according to the seasons and times of the day, discussed the techniques of playing ragas in different ways, the feeling of the melodies, and the importance of certain notes (vadi and samvadi), the grace notes and other embellishments. He talked about bhava (emotion) and explored the different aspects of rhythm. He classified the instruments that were in use at the time.

The next milestone in the medieval period was the division of Indian music into two systems, the south Indian (Carnatic) and the north Indian (Hindustani). Indian music was believed to be homogeneous throughout the country until it was subjected to external influences.

In the north, music began to change due to Arabic and Persian influences that Islamic invaders brought with them. The south remained relatively uninfluenced since the invaders did not establish their rule south of the Vindhya mountains. This gradually brought about the development of two distinct systems.

DEVELOPMENT OF CARNATIC MUSIC

While Hindustani music begin to change due to external influences, Carnatic music continued to develop along the same path as before.

Sri Vidyaranya (1320–80), the Shankaracharya of Sringeri Sharada Peetham and the founder of the Vijayanagar empire, used the term 'mela' for parent (janaka) ragas in his treatise *Sangita Sudha* for the first time. He has mentioned fifteen melas and fifty derived (janya) ragas, and the concept of sixteen swaras in an octave.

Annamacharya (1424–1503) was the eldest member of a family of composers from Tallapakkam who lived in the fifteenth century. He was a great devotee of Lord Venkateswara (a form of Vishnu and the deity in the temple on the Tirupati hills in Andhra Pradesh). He would climb the hills every day to go to the temple. There are stories that, on one occasion, the goddess Alamelumanga, consort of Venkateswara, appeared before him and blessed him.

The Tallapakkam composers (so called because they came from a small village of that name in Andhra Pradesh) were early composers in the kriti form which had three sections: pallavi, anupallavi and charanam. Annamacharya was prolific and versatile, and is believed to have written thirty thousand songs. He started composing at the age of sixteen. He wrote in Sanskrit and Telugu. His songs, which sprang forth from his great devotion, were beautiful both in musical and lyrical content.

He was the earliest composer of the kirtana and shringara padams in Telugu. It is believed that his shringara padams were the inspiration for Kshetragna's padams. Annamacharya was given the title of Padakavita Pitamaha (the grandfather of padam poetry).

Purandara Dasa (1484–1564) was born in Purandaragada to Kamalamba and Varadappa Naik. He was named Srinivasa Naik. His father was a very successful moneylender. The young Srinivasa was well-trained in music and very fluent in Sanskrit and Kannada. At the age of twenty, he married Saraswati Bai. He followed his father's profession and was well known as a miser. Legend has it that an incident involving his wife changed Purandara Dasa, leading him to a life of service to the Lord. It is said that Saraswati Bai was once approached by a poor Brahmin who needed monetary help. She gave him her diamond nose-ring, without her husband's knowledge. When the Brahmin went to pawn the nose-ring with her husband, Purandara Dasa recognised the jewel as his wife's and was furious! He locked it up in the safe in the shop, went home and asked his wife to bring him the piece of jewellery. His wife, not knowing what to do, decided it would be better to end her life. She was about to drink a cup of poison, when she noticed that the nose-ring was lying in the cupboard. She took it out gave it to her husband. Perplexed, he went back to the shop where he found that the jewel was missing from the safe. When he returned home, his wife told him the whole story and he realised that the Brahmin was none other than the Lord himself. This caused him to renounce all his worldly possessions and become a Haridasa (servant of the Lord—Hari meaning Krishna and dasa meaning servant or slave). From then on he came to be known as Purandara Dasa. He travelled all over the country visiting places of pilgrimage and composing songs on deities.

He was the most prolific of all south Indian composers. It is said that he had wanted to compose 5,00,000 songs in his lifetime. The bard says in one of his own compositions that he had composed 475,000! His devotional songs are known as Devaranamas (names of the Lord). These songs contain the very essence of the Upanishads and the Puranas. Though the language is simple, his ideas are lofty, his thoughts sublime. The mudra he used in his songs was Purandara Vittala. His invaluable contribution to music earned him the title of Karnataka Sangeeta Pitamaha (the grandfather of Carnatic music). He laid the foundation for present-day Carnatic music and brought about a major transformation by devising a method for learning south Indian music. He created the scale exercises (saralai varisai: saralai = simple, varisai = sequence), exercises to expand vocal range (tara sthayi varisai: tara = higher, sthayi = octave), and alankarams (exercises based on the seven talas). He also created simple melodic compositions in a particular raga, set to a rhythmic cycle where each syllable is set to a particular note, known as gitams. It was he who introduced Mayamalavagaula as the first scale to be learned.

Swaramelakalanidhi by Ramamatya was published in 1550. It is considered one of the most important works tracing the history of the modern period. Ramamatya discarded the grama-murchchana-jati system, describing the mela raga in clear, precise terms. He was the first to clearly classify ragas into a system of parent (janaka) and derived (janya) ragas. Venkatamakhi later built his classic scheme of the seventy-two melakartas on this. Ramamatya mentions twenty melas and sixty-four janya ragas along with its swaras. In fact, he uses the term 'mela' in the title of the treatise, *Swaramelakalanidhi,* highlighting its importance.

THE MODERN PERIOD

During the seventeenth century, Lochana in his treatise *Raga Tarangini* mentioned twelve thaats (parent scales) and seventy-eight janya (derived) ragas. He classifies them on the basis of shuddh (major), komal (minor) and tivra (augmented) swaras (notes).

Somanatha in his treatise *Raga Vibodha* (1609 CE) mentions 960 melas derived from seven shuddha swaras (pure notes) and fifteen vikrita swaras (changed notes). He further explains that only twenty-three melas were in vogue during his period, and also gives the characteristics of the melas like graha (starting note), amsha (primary note), nyasa (landing note) and time of rendering.

Kshetrajna's (1600–80) original name was Varadayya. He travelled from place to place visiting sacred places (which are known as kshetras), therefore he came to be called Kshetrayya or Kshetrajna. He was a great scholar of music and had a good command over Telugu, in which he composed. He perfected the padam to what it is today. A prolific composer, he wrote over four thousand padams. He composed in several rare ragas and the ragas he chose were always perfect for the emotions he was conveying in the particular padam. The simple beauty and appeal of the lyrics and the emotional quality of the music make his padams very moving. They deal with the themes of longing for the Lord, pangs of separation, jealousy, betrayal, using the nayaka-nayaki approach of Jayadeva.

He is believed to have been born in a village called Muvva or Muvvapuri, and was a great devotee of Gopala (another name for Krishna) who was the resident deity of his village. He chose the mudra Gopala for his compositions. His mudra appears in one of the earlier sections (pallavi, anupallavi, or charanam) of the padam, as opposed to the norm where the mudra appears in the last or charanam section. Also, in several of his padams, it is customary to start singing the composition from the second section, the anupallavi, and then come back to the first section, the pallavi. Kshetrajna's padams are still performed in both dance and music concerts.

Ventakamakhi's *Chaturdandi Prakasika* was published around 1660. This work is the basis of the present-day system of music, and deals with shrutis, swaras, ragas, talas and melas. His most significant contribution to Carnatic music is the formulation of the scheme of the seventy-two melakartas or parent scales. He worked it out scientifically applying the process of permutation and combination to the twelve notes in a scale. Venkatamakhi classified the melas but the process of naming them was completed by his grandson Muddu Venkatamakhi.

Tulaja, an eighteenth-century king of Thanjavur, wrote on melas in his treatise *Sangita Saramrita.* Along with Venkatamakhi's melas, he lists out nineteen melas which were in vogue during his days.

On the basis of Venkatamakhi's seventy-two melas, Govindacharya, the author of *Sangraha Choodamani*, outlined some more rules and formulated the melas. Govindacharya's classification is the one that is followed today.

THE GOLDEN AGE OF CARNATIC MUSIC

The eighteenth century is considered to be the golden age of Carnatic music. During this time lived three great composers/musicians who were later to be celebrated as the musical trinity: Shyama Shastri, Tyagaraja and Muthuswami Dikshitar. Their knowledge, deep spirituality, profound musicianship, creativity and innovations have made their contributions to Carnatic music invaluable.

All three of their compositions show unique styles. Tyagaraja's compositions are simple, beautiful and charming. They have universal appeal. In his compositions, he speaks the language of music in its simplest and purest form. Dikshitar's compositions, on the other hand, are very carefully worked out. They generally appeal only to the initiated few. These kritis have to be studied in detail before one can fully appreciate their value. Shyama Shastri's compositions are neither as simple as Tyagaraja's nor as complex as Dikshitar's. However, they have a unique charm of their own. Tyagaraja's compositions are said to be like grapes—they taste sweet as soon as you put them in your mouth. Shyama Shastri's compositions are compared to bananas—in order to enjoy the fruit, you have to peel the skin. Dikshitar's compositions are likened to a coconut—the fibre needs to be shucked, the nut cracked and the kernel removed.

Shyama Shastri (1762–1827), born on 26 April 1762, was the only son of Visvanatha Iyer, a temple priest. Shyama Shastri was given the name of Venkatasubramania. He was affectionately known as Shyama Krishna, which later became the mudra (signature word) in his compositions.

He was taught Sanskrit and Telugu and some music by his uncle. Since he was being groomed to become a priest, they did not concentrate too much on the music. A sanyasi (ascetic) by the name of Sangeeta Swami visited his home in Thanjavur where the family had moved when he was eighteen. Recognising his talents, the Swami took Shyama Shastri under his wing and initiated him into the intricacies of raga and tala.

According to his guru's wishes, Shyama Shastri acquainted himself with Pachimiriyam Adiyappa, who was a great musician of that time. Adiyappa was very impressed with Shyama Shastri's knowledge and had great regard for him.

Shyama Shastri was well placed in life and did not need any patronage. He was extremely religious and spent his life in the worship of Goddess Kamakshi, the deity of Kanchipuram in Tamil Nadu. He was a contemporary and good friend of Tyagaraja. In fact Shyama Shastri sent his son, Subbaraya Shastri, to study with Tyagaraja.

Shyama Shastri composed a group of nine kritis known as the *Navarathnamalika* (garland of nine gems) in the praise of Goddess Meenakshi of the Madurai temple. Of these, only seven are available today. Some of his songs are rich in rhythmic conception. He used different talas like Adi, Triputa, Rupaka, but his speciality was the misra chapu tala (seven-beat cycle). He took pleasure in composing pieces in this tala in its normal pattern (three plus four) and also in reverse four plus three. His use of different nadais like tisra and misra in his compositions show his genius as a composer.

There is a famous incident that bears testimony to Shyama Shastri's extraordinary knowledge and skill. He was once requested to take up the challenge of competing against a singer named Kesavayya who had defeated several famous musicians in competitions and was very proud of his feats. Kesavayya started by singing a pallavi in the Simhanandana tala, the longest of the one hundred and eight talas with hundred and twenty-eight beats per cycle. Shyama Shastri not only repeated it with great ease but went on to sing a pallavi in the Sarabanandana tala with seventy-nine beats to the cycle and intricate divisions, challenging Kesavayya to repeat it. This, Shyama Shastri's own creation, completely baffled Kesavayya who eventually admitted defeat!

Shyama Shastri composed in apurva (uncommon) ragas, with as much flourish as in common ragas. His compositions have a peculiar charm of their own. They are not as simple as those of Tyagaraja's but not as laboured as Dikshitar's compositions either. He is believed to have composed about three hundred songs. Most of these were kritis, though he did compose some varnams and swarajatis. He perfected the swarajati to its present form. His scholarly composition *Devi Brova* in Raga Chintamani (his own creation) shows his innovative and creative genius.

Of the trinity, Shyama Shastri's compositions are the least known. This is probably due to the fact that scholarly creations need a certain degree of proficiency to master. Also, he did not have too many disciples to popularise his compositions, many of which have been lost over time.

Tyagaraja (1767–1847) was born on 4 May 1767 in Tiruvarur. He was named Tyagaraja after the deity of Tiruvarur. In his compositions, he used his name as his mudra.

Tyagaraja lived most of his life in Tiruvayyar on the banks of the Kaveri river in a house that the king of Thanjavur had gifted his father, Ramabrahmam. It was a great seat of learning which went on to produce several saints and musicians. Tyagaraja learnt Sanskrit and Telugu from his father. He learnt several compositions of composers like Purandara Dasa from his mother, Seetamma. He then took lessons from Sonti Venkataramana Das who was a musician in the Thanjavur court.

Tyagaraja was a prolific composer with over two thousand songs to his credit. His compositions were mostly in Telugu though he did compose in Sanskrit as well. He is credited with evolving and perfecting the kriti form. The concept of the sangati (melodic variations on a line in the composition used to beautify it) was his contribution. Besides numerous kritis, he also wrote two musical dramas, *Prahlada Bhakti Vijayam* and *Nauka Charitram*.

Tyagaraja was a great devotee of Rama and his songs are noble, sublime and soul-stirring. He placed great importance and emphasis on the value of truly spiritual music. His style is simple, appealing to scholar and layman alike.

Tyagaraja wrote several songs in uncommon, unusual ragas. He also composed songs in lesser-used melakarta ragas. His pancharatna kritis (pancha means five and ratna means jewel or gem) are in a class by themselves. They are based on the five ghana ragas: Nattai, Gaulai, Arabhi, Varali and Sri. Unusual in form, they consist of pallavi, anupallavi and multiple charanams. The charanams are first sung with swarams and then repeated with the lyrics.

Tyagaraja composed mostly in the Adi tala, though he did use a few other talas like Rupaka, Misra chapu, Kanda chapu, the Desadi and Madhyadi talas. He was the first composer to popularise songs with the anagata eduppu, compositions starting after the first or the downbeat, for example, ¼ beat, ½ beat, ¾ beat and 1½ beats after the samam (downbeat). Till his time, most compositions had a sama eduppu that started on the downbeat.

Tyagaraja is said to have had the largest number of disciples in

India's musical history. These disciples propagated and popularised his music. Several of his disciples became great composers.

Tyagaraja passed away on 6 January 1847 in Tiruvayyar. A memorial erected in his honour is today treated as a sacred spot. It is a place of pilgrimage for musicians, music-lovers and devotees alike. Every year, in January, around the day that Tyagaraja died, the Tyagaraja Aradhana festival is held in Tiruvayyar. Attended by thousands, the festival draws top-ranking artists. On the last day, everyone gathered there, musicians and music-lovers alike, sing the pancharatna kritis in unison.

Muthuswami Dikshitar (1775–1835), born on 24 March 1775 in the city of Tiruvarur in Thanjavur district, was the youngest of the trinity. He came from a family of distinguished musicians. His father, Ramaswami Dikshitar, was a great scholar and composer, who is credited with having created Raga Hamsadhwani. Muthuswami's brother, Baluswami Dikshitar, is believed to be the first Indian who learnt the violin and adapted it to Indian music. Muthuswami learnt music and the Telugu and Sanskrit languages from his father. By the time he was sixteen, he was proficient in music, the Vedas, the Upanishads, astrology and mythology. His compositions are proof of his profound knowledge in all these subjects.

When the family was living in a town called Manali, about twenty miles from Tiruvarur, Muthuswami met Chidambara Yogi, a spiritual teacher. Muthuswami accompanied the great saint to Varanasi, on the banks of the Ganges. He lived there for five years and mastered Sanskrit and Tantric Yoga, learning many shastras (sciences). There, he was evidently drawn to the north Indian dhrupad style of singing and incorporated it in some of his compositions, which are comparatively slow-paced. He also composed several songs in north Indian ragas (for example, the kriti *Akhilandeshwari* in Raga Dwijavanti, which is similar to the north Indian Raga Jaijaivanti).

He travelled widely to sacred places of worship. In Tiruttani (near present-day Chennai), he was blessed with a vision of Muruga, his favourite deity. It is said that Lord Subramanya appeared to

Muthuswami in human form, put some sweets into his mouth and then disappeared. Muthuswami then composed his first kriti and appropriately chose the name Guruguha (another name for Muruga, also called Skanda or Subramanya) as his mudra.

His Navagraha kritis in praise of the nine planets reveal his knowledge of astrology. Originally, they were known as the vara kritis (vara meaning week) and were seven in number, one for each day of the week, based on the seven basic talas. The other two in praise of Rahu and Ketu were added later to make them nine in number. His Navavarana kritis in praise of the Devi (Parvati), one for each of the nine days of the Navaratri festival, are superb examples of his scholarly compositions.

He sang kritis in praise of all deities. His songs are normally slow in tempo and bring out the depth and beauty of the raga with much use of ornamentation (gamakas). In a typical kriti, he often used a madhyama kala (medium tempo) passage, faster in tempo (typically double) than the rest of the song. This enhanced the beauty of the composition. He composed songs in many rare ragas and talas, revealing great intellectual capacity. The carefully worked out, laboured quality of his works appeals more to a listener initiated in Carnatic music.

In 1835, on Deepavali day (the festival of lights), Muthuswami Dikshitar passed away, as his brother and disciples sang one of his outstanding compositions, *Meenakshi Me Mudam*, in Raga Purvikalyani.

Dikshitar, during the early part of his life (because of the influence of his family patron, Venkatakrishna Mudaliyar), was exposed to Western music, adapted Western melodies, and created what are now called 'nottuswarams', using Sanskrit text. (The word 'nottuswaram' is an interesting usage that comes from 'note' + 'swaram' both of which mean the same thing.) Even though Western and north Indian influences were evident, he still retained the identity of south Indian classical music, in a way creating even heavier south Indian classical compositions by fusing western and north Indian concepts. This gives him the special honour of being the first 'fusion' composer.

Swati Tirunal (1813–46), the king of Travancore in Kerala, was born on 16 April 1813. He was the second child of the queen of Travancore, Rani Gowri Lakshmi Bayi and Raja Raja Varma Koyil Thampuran. He was born under the star Swati, one of the twenty-seven stars in the Indian system of astrology. Swati Tirunal's mother died while he was still an infant and he was brought up by his aunt, Rani Parvati Bai. She played a very important role in his lofty achievements.

Swati Tirunal was crowned at the age of sixteen. Since he was groomed to become a king, he was trained in various areas in which a king was expected to be proficient. He was fluent enough in thirteen languages to be able to write poems and songs in them! He was also well-versed in other arts like painting and sculpture, and was a great patron of the arts.

Swati Tirunal was a good ruler who had the welfare of his subjects at heart. His vision and his reforms made his reign, short though it was, an important one in history. He was responsible for building in Travancore the first English school, a public library, an observatory, a press and so on. He improved conditions for foreign trade and undertook several social reforms to alleviate the suffering of women. In the second half of his reign, he faced problems with the British ruling India at the time and this, along with the deaths of his sister and nephew, affected him deeply. Thereafter, he shied away from the world and withdrew into his music.

He passed away at the young age of thirty-three but not before making a great contribution to Carnatic music, that is, the five hundred-odd songs that he is believed to have composed. Besides varnams, swarajatis, padams and javalis, he also wrote two musical dramas. He also composed dhrupads, khyals, tappas, thumris and bhajans in the Hindustani style. He used the mudra Padmanabha (Vishnu) in honour of the resident deity of Travancore.

Swati Tirunal had in his court disciples of Tyagaraja and

Muthuswami Dikshitar. He was keen to meet Tyagaraja and since he could not free himself of his royal duties, he sent a court musician to request the great bard to grace his court. Tyagaraja, who declined the invitation, sent a message to the king that they would certainly meet in another world.

Swati Tirunal passed away on 26 December 1846. It is commendable that despite all his royal duties and the problems he faced in his personal life and as a monarch, he was still able to compose such a variety of beautiful, inspired songs.

Patnam Subramania Iyer (1845–1902) was not only a great composer but also a great performer. He was the disciple of Manambuchavadi Venkatasubbayyar, who in turn was a disciple of Tyagaraja. He was very well-known and honoured by several patrons and kings for his great talent. His compositions, which total around a hundred, include kritis, tana varnams, pada varnams, javalis and tillanas. Most of his compositions are in Telugu, but he also wrote in Sanskrit and Tamil. He had a superb style that reveals his genius as a composer. His compositions are extremely popular and performed a lot. He used the mudras Venkateswara, Varada Venkateswara or slight variations of the two.

Mysore Vasudevacharya (1865–1961) wrote more than two hundred compositions, mostly in Sanskrit and Telugu. He was a disciple of Patnam Subramania Iyer, among others. He was respected as a great scholar apart from being an accomplished singer and composer. For a while, he taught at the Kalakshetra in Chennai, working on an ambitious project of setting the Ramayana to music. Later, Government of India honoured him with the Padma Bhushan.

Koteeswara Iyer (1869–1938) was one of the first musicians to compose in all seventy-two melakarta ragas. Koteeswara was the grandson of Kavi Kunjara Bharathi and used the mudra Kavi Kunjara Dasan in his honour.

Harikesanallur Muthiah Bhagavathar (1877–1945) was born to Lingamayyar and Anandam Ammal. He was a student of the Vedas in Tiruvayyar. It is said that when he heard the music of Maha

Vaidyanatha Iyer and Patnam Subramania Iyer, he got so deeply affected that he gave up his Vedic studies and began concentrating on music. His debut concert in 1897 was held in the presence of the king of Travancore. Bhagavathar composed in Sanskrit, Telugu, Tamil and Kannada in several rare ragas as well as varnams, kritis, tillanas and ragamalikas. He used the mudra Harikesa. He also did much to popularise Swati Tirunal's compositions. He received a doctorate in 1943 for his work *Sangeeta Kalpadruma* which deals with the theory of music.

Papanasam Sivan (1890–1973) born in Polaham in the Thanjavur district on 26 September 1890, was the second son of Ramamruta Iyer and his wife Yogambal. He was named Ramayyah at birth. At the age of seven, he lost his father and moved with his mother and brother to Trivandrum where he studied Sanskrit. He received his early music training from Noorani Mahadeva Bhagavathar and Samba Bhagavathar. He was also greatly influenced by the famous singer Konerirajapuram Vaidyanatha Iyer.

A prolific composer, Papanasam Sivan wrote about two thousand and five hundred songs in a wide variety of ragas. He composed in Tamil and Sanskrit. He composed for and performed in theatrical productions, both as a singer and actor, and taught at the Kalakshetra from 1934 to 1939. He started composing for movies in 1935 and later, also acted in four movies. Many national awards and honours were conferred on him, including the Padma Bhushan and the fellowship of the Sangeet Natak Akademi.

Here is a brief (though not exhaustive) list of some of the other important composers of the Carnatic tradition:

Bhadrachala Ramdas (1620–80)
Narayana Tirtha (1650–1745)
Ramaswami Dikshitar (1735–1817)
Vina Kuppayyar (1798–1860)
Pacchimiriam Adiappayya (eighteenth century)
Pallavi Gopala Iyer (eighteenth century)

Sadashiva Brahmendra (eighteenth century)
Subbaraya Shastry (1803–62)
Chengalvaraya Shastry (1810–1900)
Kavi Kunjara Bharati (1810–96)
Gopalakrishna Bharati (1810–96)
Annaswami Shastry (nineteenth century)
Ghanam Krishna Iyer (nineteenth century)
Anayya (nineteenth century)
Dharmapuri Subbarayar (nineteenth century)
Karur Dakshinamurti Shastry (nineteenth century)
Muvvalur Sabhapati Iyer (nineteenth century)
Mysore Sadashiva Rao (nineteenth century)
Ponnayya Pillai (1804–64)
Nilakantha Sivan (1839–1900)
Subbarama Dikshitar (1839–1906)
Pallavi Sheshayyar (1842–1909)
Maha Vaidyanatha Iyer (1844–93)
Tiruvottriyur Tyagayyar (1845–1917)
Ramnad Srinivasa Iyengar (1860–1919)
Annamalai Reddiyar (1865–91)
Subramania Bharati (1882–1921)
Subbarama Bhagavathar (twentieth century)
Professor V. Lakshminarayana (1911–90)
M. Balamuralikrishna (1930–2016)[2]

INTRODUCTION TO NORTH INDIAN MUSIC

To understand and discuss North Indian classical music (also known as Hindustani music), it is important to learn about the contributions made by eminent personalities in this field. Here are a few renowned North Indian musicians:

[2] Information about some of these composers has been included in the Appendix.

Amir Khusrau was born in 1253 AD in Patiala. His father was an official in the Delhi Sultanate, serving Shams'ud'din Il'tutmish. Khusrau learnt Persian, theology, Qur'an and other subjects even as a young boy. His mother hailed from India and it is from his maternal line (from his mother and his maternal grandfather) that he picked up the local languages and also became intimate with the culture of Hindustan.

When Khusrau was twenty years old, he started his career as a professional writer/poet, composing songs and poems in exalted praise of the Sultan. He started out as a court poet for some of the noblemen and slowly graduated to the courts of princes and finally moved to the durbar of the Sultan himself. He was made a permanent court poet and held that post for five decades until his death in 1325. It was Khusrau who fused Indian, Turkish, Persian, and Arabic music to create a new genre of music in the thirteenth century—the qawwali, a form of devotional music associated with the Sufis.

Khusrau travelled widely, met several people, observed nature, studied the cultures and learnt the languages, which gave him a broad understanding of Hindu culture and traditions. His major writings include the *Tuhfat al-Sighar* (poems of adolescence), *Wasat al-Hayāt* (poems of middle life), *Ghurrat al-Kamāl* (poems of maturity, c. 1293), *Baqiyya-yi-Naqiyya* (c. 1315), and *Nihāyat al-Kamāl*. In addition, he wrote the *Matlā al-Anwār, Shirīn-i-Khusrau, Majnūn-Laylā, Āīnā-yi-Sikandarī* and *Hasht Bihisht.*

Tansen (1500–86), who was also known as Ramtanu Pandey, was a famous exponent of Hindustani music. He was born in a musical family and perfected his art in the region that lies between modern-day Madhya Pradesh and Rajasthan. He was a student of Swami Haridas, who is said to have been a disciple of Purandara Dasa. He started out his career and spent a greater part of his professional life in the court of the Hindu king of Rewa, Raja Ramachandra Singh (who ruled from 1555 to 1592). It was there that his musical prowess gained widespread fame and reached Delhi, where Akbar was ruling. Legend has it that Akbar sent messengers to Raja Ramchandra Singh asking him to send Tansen to his court. Although Tansen was unwilling, it was Raja Ramchandra Singh who encouraged him to go to Delhi in order to gain a wider audience. Sometime in the 1560s, Tansen joined the court of Akbar and became one of the nine jewels of his court. Apart from being a remarkable singer, Tansen was also a composer and helped popularise the use of musical instruments. He created new ragas, composed famous Dhrupad compositions and also wrote a few books on music, like *Sri Ganesh Stotra* and *Sangita Sara*.

Vishnu Narayan Bhatkhande (1860–1936) was a renowned musicologist who was among the first to write a treatise that dealt with the theoretical aspects of Hindustani music. Although Hindustani music had been around for over four hundred years, it didn't have a structured framework. It was propagated through oral tradition, and would, therefore, undergo a lot of change based on the creativity of different performers. Eventually, the raga grammar that had been laid out in the older works became outdated. Earlier, the ragas were divided into ragas (masculine), raginis (feminine) and putra (offspring). Taking inspiration from the melakarta system created by the Carnatic musicologist and composer Venkatamakhi, Bhatkhande classified the ragas into thaats. He created the now-prevalent system of ten thaats. Ragas that were in vogue were sung in a manner totally different from their descriptions in ancient treatises. Bhatkhande explained the characteristics of the ragas in a simple manner and also composed several bandishes that helped explain the grammar of the raga. He borrowed the concept of the lakshana geetham from Venkatamakhi. Bhatkhande travelled widely in India, meeting with several great musicians, and in parallel began a rigorous study of ancient works such as the *Natyashastra* and *Sangita Ratnakara*. He also developed a modern notation system for Hindustani music.

THE POST-INDEPENDENCE PERIOD

Most Indian musicologists stop at the nineteenth century when talking about the history of music. But I would like to express a few thoughts about the recent past, the present and the future. Since the golden age, there have been innovations in the different styles of music created by different masters. Some instruments like the violin, which were earlier used more as accompanying instruments, have gained prominence and developed into solo instruments. Here I must mention that it was my father and guru, Professor V. Lakshminarayana, who was responsible for making the violin a solo instrument in Carnatic music by introducing original masterful techniques of playing and interpreting the vocal repertoire in violin-playing. The violin that is presently used in all Indian music was first adapted to Carnatic music during the British period. Similarly, in recent years, many Western instruments like the guitar, mandolin, clarinet and saxophone have been successfully introduced and adapted to Indian music. Generally, Indian classical music is almost always performed in concert halls and festivals using amplification. Some instrumentalists have been using contact microphones for quite some time. There has been tremendous improvement in the quality and virtuosity in the field of instruments during this century. Music has become much more accessible and some of the Indian classical music festivals now attract larger audiences, not only in India but around the world. In many music festivals, lecture-demonstrations and discussions are common features. Nowadays, it is not uncommon for people to enjoy more than one genre of music—be it Indian classical, Western, East–West fusion or film music.

There has been a wider acceptance of Carnatic music in the latter half of this century within India. Before this time, performances were limited to the four southern states of Tamil Nadu, Andhra Pradesh, Karnataka and Kerala. Though there were concerts of Carnatic music in other parts of India, they were conducted mostly by south Indian organisations (generally known as sabhas). Though it was customary to invite Hindustani musicians to perform in Carnatic music festivals, the reverse was rare.

Around the first half of the twentieth century, some Hindustani musicians and musicologists started taking an interest in, and tried to understand, the extremely complex nature of the rhythmic structure and the melodic concept of Carnatic music. Some of the ragas of the south were also adapted and performed by the great Hindustani performers. The reverse, that is, the adaptation of Hindustani ragas into the Carnatic system had started much earlier, around two centuries ago. During his time, the great composer Muthuswami Dikshitar had travelled in the north and composed songs in several Hindustani ragas. In fact, it was not uncommon to hear a bhajan (a Hindustani musical form) performed in a Carnatic concert.

Another recent development has been the evolution of the Hindustani–Carnatic jugalbandi (a duet). The jugalbandi was common in the Hindustani tradition earlier. This traditionally meant a duet between two musicians, vocal or instrumental. It was more commonly performed by brothers or musicians who were students of the same guru and belonged to the same gharana (style of music). This is not necessarily so now. There are jugalbandis of various artists of different styles and unusual combinations of instruments. In the Hindustani–Carnatic jugalbandi,[3] as the name implies, two artists, one from each tradition, come together to perform. There have been occasions where a Hindustani percussionist has accompanied a Carnatic performer (together with one or more Carnatic accompanists) and vice versa. Some of these novelties have been very successful. Also, the concept of the percussion ensemble (tala vadya), which is a part of the southern tradition, has been adapted in the north using both north and south Indian percussion instruments. Similarly, konnakol (using the voice as a percussion instrument by reciting percussive syllables) in a music performance,

3 The first instance of a Carnatic–Hindustani jugalbandi was perhaps the one that I played with Ustad Ali Akbar Khan in the 1970s.

a practice in the Carnatic tradition, has also been adapted in the north.

Due to growth in mass media communication and an increase in global travel, the public is now better exposed to different cultures and performing arts. This is also due to advanced technology and the wide-spread availability of music from different parts of the world in the form of audio and video recordings.

Because of these factors, it is now possible for Indian performers to establish themselves internationally, provided they take into account the perceptions, expectations and the understanding of the international audience and meet the resultant challenges with innovation, creativity and musicianship. They are in competition with several great international performers from other cultures in order to be successful.

In the coming years, one can probably expect more instruments from other cultures to be introduced and adapted to the Indian system. Greater modification of existing instruments is also possible. In the 1980s, I was one of the first to experiment with a violin synthesiser (developed by Keith McMillen) which, through a MIDI connection, triggered one or more keyboard synthesisers, thereby tapping hundreds of sounds that were available through those keyboards.

In the field of musical composition, there have been many attempts at East–West compositions where the composer has drawn on Eastern and Western concepts and musicians from both traditions have performed together. I created the Global Fusion idiom in the 1970s with a view to integrate different musical forms and also to give a legitimate place to Indian classical music in the global arena.

One can expect more and more innovative efforts in the years to come, resulting in a global fusion in the field of experimental music in which I have been working for the past five decades. This has also brought different artistes together, and in turn, a mutual love and respect for different traditions and cultures has emerged which is very essential for peace and harmony in our society.

2

The Elements of Music

The underlying unity and the ability to integrate musical styles comes from the fact that in any system of music around the world, there are two basic concepts: melodic and rhythmic. Both these concepts complement each other to create music.

The fundamental unit of a melody is called a 'note' in the West and a 'swara' in Indian classical music. When a number of notes are arranged systematically, they form a scale. The fundamental unit of rhythm is a 'beat'. When a number of beats come together systematically, they form a rhythmic cycle (tala).

In terms of structure, the basic melodic idea in Indian classical music is called a 'raga'. In Western classical music, it is the 'scale'. Similarly, the basic rhythmic idea in Indian classical music is called 'tala'. In Western classical music, the rhythmic cycle is indicated by a time signature, which is denoted by a fraction. The number above indicates the number of beats in a bar and the number below indicates the duration of the note or what type of beat it is. For example, 2/4 indicates there will be two beats in a bar and the type of beat will be quarter notes (or 'crotchets') since four crotchets make a whole note. Also, in the West, the tempo is often indicated at the beginning of the composition. For example, if a crotchet is equal to forty counts, it indicates that the tempo will be forty crotchets in a minute.

Typically, music has seven notes (swaras). In Indian classical music, we call them:

Shadja
Rishabha
Gandhara
Madhyama
Panchama
Dhaivata
Nishada

While singing, we say:

Sa
Ri / Re
Ga
Ma
Pa
Dha
Ni

While notating Indian classical music, we use the first letters of the notes alone:

S
R
G
M
P
D
N

In the Western classical system, the first seven letters of the English alphabet are used to denote the seven notes. But we also have the Solfège system, which uses:

Do
Re
Mi
Fa
So
La
Ti

While notating Western classical music, we use what is called a 'staff notation'. This consists of five horizontal parallel lines which have the clef mark at the beginning (on the extreme left). This determines the position of the notes on the staves. In other words, it indicates the pitch of the notes written on the staves. If we use the 'treble clef' (or G-clef), the note on the second line from the bottom is the G. If we use the 'bass clef' (or the F-clef), the note on the second line from the top is F. We also have the 'alto clef', 'tenor clef' and so forth.

There are four basic scales in Western classical music:

1. Major scale, which has the following notes: tonic, major second, major third, perfect fourth, perfect fifth, major sixth and major seventh. This corresponds to the scale of the Raga Shankarabharanam in south Indian classical music.
2. Minor scale, which is of three types in general:
   a) Natural Minor: tonic, major second, minor third, perfect fourth, perfect fifth, minor sixth and minor seventh. This corresponds to the scale of the Raga Natabhairavi in south Indian classical music.
   b) Harmonic Minor: tonic, major second, minor third, perfect fourth, perfect fifth, minor sixth and major seventh. This corresponds to the scale of the Raga Kiravani in south Indian classical music.
   c) Melodic Minor: In the ascent, it has tonic, major second, minor third, perfect fourth, perfect fifth, major sixth and major seventh while in the descent it has minor seventh,

minor sixth, perfect fifth, perfect fourth, minor third, major second and tonic. The ascent of this scale corresponds to the scale of the Raga Gourimanohari and the descent of this scale corresponds to the scale of the Raga Natabhairavi.

These four scales can be played in each of the twelve semitones, so we get a total of forty-eight scales in Western classical music.

Apart from the four basic scales, Western classical music also has a system of modes. There are seven modes:

1. Ionian mode, which corresponds to the major scale (i.e. scale of the Raga Shankarabharanam/Bilawal)
2. Dorian mode: tonic, major second, minor third, perfect fourth, perfect fifth, major sixth and minor seventh. This corresponds to the scale of the Raga Kharaharapriya/Kafi.
3. Phrygian mode: tonic, minor second, minor third, perfect fourth, perfect fifth, minor sixth and minor seventh. This corresponds to the scale of the Raga Hanumatodi/Bhairavi.
4. Lydian mode: tonic, major second, major third, augmented fourth, perfect fifth, major sixth and major seventh. This corresponds to the scale of the Raga Mechakalyani/Kalyan.
5. Mixolydian mode: tonic, major second, major third, perfect fourth, perfect fifth, major sixth and minor seventh. This corresponds to the scale of the Raga Harikambhoji/Khammaj.
6. Aeolian mode, which corresponds to the natural minor scale (i.e. scale of the Raga Natabhairavi/Asavari).
7. Locrian mode: tonic, minor second, minor third, perfect fourth, diminished fifth, minor sixth and minor seventh. There is no corresponding scale in the traditional scheme of south Indian classical music.

All these modes can be played in each of the twelve semitones, so we get sixty new scales (since two of the modes have already been covered in the previous set of four scales). In total, it can be said that there are a hundred and eight different scales available in Western classical music.

In south Indian classical music, we have seventy-two parent scales, known as the 'melakartas'.

In north Indian classical music, there are ten parent scales, which are called 'thaats'.

The basic seven-note system is further divided into twelve semitones and enharmonically, we get a total of sixteen notes.

3

The Notation System

The notation system in Indian music is not complete enough to notate all the delicate nuances, ornamentations (collectively called gamakas) and microtones (shrutis), which are its very essence. It is because of these very ornamentations and microtones, whose interpretations vary from performer to performer and teacher to teacher, that it is almost impossible to come up with a notation system perfect enough to do the job. Further, the music, which evolved from the Vedas, was passed down from generation to generation by oral tradition for hundreds of years. In this guru–shishya parampara (teacher–student tradition), the student would learn music on a one-on-one basis from the guru. The music was never notated or written down until much later, mainly as a memory aid. Even so, it was only a skeletal representation. To this day, students are discouraged from singing or playing their instruments while looking at the book which has the musical notations. Rather, they are expected to listen to the guru, to repeat the lesson and memorise it, and then play from memory. Many great performers of the past were products of the guru–shishya parampara and learning from a guru is considered the most effective way of learning Indian classical music.

Working with gurus in this manner helped their students develop a good memory and ear-training; teaching them to listen and repeat different notes in different pitches, including microtones and ornamentations. This helped students develop the improvisational techniques characteristic of Indian classical music. Instead of depending on a notation book or music sheets, students would concentrate and develop the capacity to listen, and learn to imitate their teachers. Also, when the guru performed, the student would accompany the guru and either play the drone instrument (tambura or shruti-peti) or keep the tala cycle. Constant listening enabled students to carefully observe the various aspects of music like the pitch, rhythm, ornamentations, dynamics, pauses and microtones, which cannot be completely captured in written notation.

The process of learning with the guru in this manner also helps accompanists and instrumental soloists. Ear-training is most essential for success as a good accompanist, someone who is expected to listen to and repeat what the main artist sings. Even when a singer presents new ragas without warning at a concert, the accompanist, with good ear-training and musicianship, is often able to repeat the raga, sometimes without even knowing the name of the raga or raga lakshana (characteristics of the raga). This is called lakshya jnana, meaning knowledge picked up through observing or listening. In Indian music, the accompanists are sometimes independently engaged by concert organisers, and in rare cases, even without the main and the accompanying artists knowing each other. They might meet for the first time just prior to the concert, only to quickly tune up and go on stage. In many cases, the main artist might not even inform the accompanist of the repertoire of the concert! There have been instances where the main artist has performed difficult ragas or used complex rhythmic structures in the swara-kalpana, after a great deal of preparation at home, and the poor accompanist is expected to cope with him on the spot! Some great accompanists have risen to the challenge and, in some instances, they have even outshone the main artist, thanks to their strong ear-training, musicianship and lakshya jnana. Ear-training is not confined only to the melodic structure. It also applies to the rhythmic aspects. There have been situations where the main artists have prepared rhythmically complex pallavis (in the ragam-tanam-pallavi portion) in difficult or uncommon talas and, after singing the pallavi in tri-kala (three different tempi), have immediately signalled (with great generosity!) to the mridangam accompanist to play a solo. Whenever the legendary Palghat T.S. Mani Iyer, the mridangam wizard, was the accompanist, he was able to not only immediately repeat the complex structure of the pallavi but, at times, would also add his own, more complicated, improvisational variations to it. This is possible only when one has superb technical control of the instrument, intuitive understanding of rhythm and a fantastic memory for the rhythmic structure.

Living and travelling with the guru helps the student develop presence of mind to tackle different problems that arose on a concert platform. The student gains important first-hand practical knowledge which cannot be learnt from a book or in any other way. This experience also helps the student acquire knowledge while in training, as opposed to learning the hard way during the performance. The disciple, sitting behind the mridangam player on stage, carries the instruments and prepares them (that is, making the cream of wheat paste to be applied to the left head of the mridangam). He also keeps the tala cycle for his guru. It helps him obtain valuable, practical experience and understand different rhythmic patterns and compositional structures that the guru plays. Sometimes the guru would even play the composition with variations, thus opening the mind of the students for greater creativity.

It is always advisable for students, when they practise alone, to practise with a tambura (drone instrument) that helps them to sing or play 'in correct pitch' or, in other words, help them develop an excellent intonation. Practising with a tambura helps one to almost 'memorise' the tonic or the basic tone Sa, which in turn, gives an intuitive sense of accurate intonation for different intervals. This is one of the essential factors in an advanced stage for the interpretation of ragas, especially because of the use of microtones and ornamentations associated with certain notes in certain ragas. Unlike Western music, we do not use the tempered scale of tuning. In recent years, some modern composers in the West have experimented with using microtones in their compositions and have tried to retune the piano to perform these pieces. Some melodic percussion instruments like marimbas have been constructed as microtonal instruments by varying the lengths of the strips of wood. Thus, there has been constant growth and innovation in different kinds of music, thanks either to the genius of some musicians and composers or to exposure to other systems of the world or, at times, on account of a combination of both these two factors.

In the case of Western music, the whole learning process is very different from that of the Indian system. Since there is a notation system that is adequate for the type of music played and there is little or no improvisation in the Western classical music tradition now, learning in musical institutions works well. In earlier times, like in the Baroque period, improvisation was a part of the tradition and later, in orchestral compositions like concertos the soloists were also expected to improvise in the cadenza sections. This was probably due to the fact that many great composers such as Bach, Mozart, Paganini, Chopin were also great performers and vice versa. However, with the passage of time, performing and composing have separated and the art of improvising, in the classical tradition, has practically disappeared. Composers write down every note that they want the performers to play. This will, hopefully, change in the future, as improvisation enhances the creativity of the performer.

A student of music in the West is taught to read musical notation and practise with it right from the beginning. Later on, at an advanced stage, this helps the student memorise compositions and play them from memory so that s/he can concentrate on other musical aspects like interpretation and intonation.

In Western music, there are people who are said to have 'perfect pitch', in other words, these are people who have the memory of a particular frequency (musical note) or, in some cases, more than one. This could become a disadvantage, especially if one is a soloist with perfect pitch and has to perform with different orchestras. Each orchestra may be tuned to the note A at a slightly different frequency; for example, if one has 'perfect pitch' for the note A with a frequency of 440, and one might not be able to play with an orchestra tuned to a frequency other than A-440. In the case of Indian music, the ear is trained in such a way that it remembers the relative intervals in relation to the basic tonic or adhara shadja. Due to this, the student develops skills in remembering the microtones (which are less than the semitones, the shortest interval in a regular keyboard) in relation to any tonic note.

Like any other system of music, there are only seven basic notes in the octave in Indian music. The seven notes are denoted by seven letters (S, R, G, M, P, D and N) like Western music, which uses the first seven letters of the alphabet (A, B, C, D, E, F and G). But each of these seven letters in Western music refers to a specific pitch. Different symbols (clef signs) are used on the staff lines (the five parallel, horizontal lines on which the symbols of the note are written) to determine the pitch, for example:

In Indian music, the letters themselves are used in the notation, but they do not denote any specific pitch since the 'S' or tonic (the basic note) known as adhara shadja (adhara, in Sanskrit, means support) is variable in pitch according to the performer's choice and the other notes are always in relation to the basic tonic.

The seven notes or saptaswaras as they are known in Indian music, are as follows:

TABLE 3.1

Swara Name	*Written*	*Pronounced*	*Corresponding Western Name*
Shadja	S	Sa	First Degree (Tonic): Do
Rishabha	R	Ri (Re in Hindustani)	Second Degree (Supertonic): Re
Gandhara	G	Ga	Third Degree (Median): Mi

Swara Name	*Written*	*Pronounced*	*Corresponding Western Name*
Madhyama	M	Ma	Fourth Degree (Subdominant): Fa
Panchama	P	Pa	Fifth Degree (Dominant): So
Dhaivata	D	Da (Dha in Hindustani)	Sixth Degree (Submediant): La
Nishada	N	Ni	Leading Note: Ti

Thus, while notating, only the first letters of the names of the notes are used, that is, S, R, G, M, P, D, N but, when reading from the notation, they are read as Sa, Ri (Re), Ga, Ma, Pa, Da (Dha) and Ni respectively.

The Indian notation system is linear in form as opposed to the staff notation system of the West. Hence, it is not visually obvious whether a note is higher or lower than another note unless you read it, while in Western music one can easily distinguish a higher note by its higher placement on one staff. For example:

It is obvious, looking at it, that the B is higher than the F, whereas if you see the Indian notes N and M, it is impossible to tell, whether the second note M is higher or lower than the first note N unless you read the notes. In general, in Indian music a note with a dot above it is always one octave higher than a note without a dot.

The main difference between the two systems is that when in Western music you say A, it always refers to a particular pitch, but in Indian music Sa only refers to the tonic or first degree, which can be any pitch. The performer has the option to choose any suitable pitch as his tonic Sa. For example, a male singer might have pitch C as his tonic (Sa), a female singer pitch G as her tonic (Sa), a violinist

D sharp as his tonic (Sa), and so on. Hence, Sa always indicates the tonic which may be any pitch. Pa stands for the perfect fifth (or dominant) above the tonic. The Pa is always a perfect fifth in relation to the Sa as Indian music does not admit the concept of a diminished or augmented fifth (that is, a lower or raised fifth). Thus, Sa and Pa are always constant. They are changeless swaras or notes that have no variations. The other five notes, Ri, Ga, Ma, Da and Ni, may be either lowered or raised.

In Carnatic music thus, Sa and Pa are always fixed, the Ma (or the fourth degree) can be of two types, while the Ri, Ga, Da and Ni can be of three types. Here's an example of the notes if the tonic or the Sa is tuned to C.

TABLE 3.2

Carnatic Name	*Carnatic Symbol*	*Western Name*	*Western Note if Sa is C*
Shadja	S	Tonic	C
Shuddha Rishabha	R_1	Minor Second	D flat
Chatusshruti Rishabha	R_2	Major Second	D natural
Shatshruti Rishabha	R_3	Augmented Second	D sharp
Shuddha Gandhara	G_1	Diminished Third	E double flat
Sadharana Gandhara	G_2	Minor Third	E flat
Antara Gandhara	G_3	Major Third	E natural
Shuddha Madhyama	M_1	Perfect Fourth	F natural
Prati Madhyama	M_2	Augmented Fourth	F sharp
Panchama	P	Perfect Fifth	G natural
Shuddha Dhaivata	D_1	Minor Sixth	A flat
Chatusshruti Dhaivata	D_2	Major Sixth	A natural
Shatshruti Dhaivata	D_3	Augmented Sixth	A sharp
Shuddha Nishada	N_1	Diminished Seventh	B double flat
Kaisiki Nishada	N_2	Minor Seventh	B flat
Kakali Nishada	N_3	Major Seventh	B natural

Carnatic music, like Western music, has the concept of enharmonic notes. Though there are only twelve semitones, there are sixteen names.

Ri (Rishabha):
- R_1 (D flat)
- R_2 (D natural) = G_1 (E double flat)
- R_3 (D sharp) = G_2 (E flat)

Ga (Gandhara):
- G_1 (E double flat)
- G_2 (E flat)
- G_3 (E natural)

Similarly,

Dha (Dhaivata):
- D_1 (A flat)
- D_2 (A natural) = N_1 (B double flat)
- D_3 (A sharp) = N_2 (B flat)

Ni (Nishada):
- N_1 (B double flat)
- N_2 (B flat)
- N_3 (B natural)

TABLE 3.3

Note	*Symbol*	*Name*	*Western Tonality* (with C as tonic)
SA	S	1. Shadja	C
	R_1	2. Shuddha Rishabha	D flat
RI	R_2	3. Chatusshruti Rishabha	D natural
	R_3	4. Shatshruti Rishabha	D sharp
	G_1	5. Shuddha Gandhara	E double flat
GA	G_2	6. Sadharana Gandhara	E flat
	G_3	7. Antara Gandhara	E natural
MA	M_1	8. Shuddha Madhyama	F natural
	M_2	9. Prati Madhyama	F sharp

Tonality wise:

$R_2 = G_1$ (like D natural = E double flat)
$R_3 = G_2$ (D sharp = E flat)
$D_2 = N_1$ (A natural = B double flat)
$D_3 = N_2$ (A sharp = B Flat)

The notes $R_{3,}$ $G_{1,}$ D_3 and N_1 are called 'Vivadhi' swaras.

Hindustani music does not have this concept of Vivadhi swaras or enharmonic notes. As a result, in Hindustani music there are two possibilities for Re, Ga, Ma, Dha and Ni.

TABLE 3.4

Hindustani Name	*Hindustani Symbol*	*Western Name*	*Western Note if Sa is C*
Shadja	S	Tonic	C
Komal Rishabha	$\underline{R}$	Minor Second	D flat
Shuddha Rishabha	R	Major Second	D natural
Komal Gandhara	$\underline{G}$	Minor Third	E flat
Shuddha Gandhara	G	Major Third	E natural
Shuddha Madhyama	M	Perfect Fourth	F natural
Tivra Madhyama	$\overset{\mid}{M}$	Augmented Fourth	F sharp
Panchama	P	Perfect Fifth	G natural
Komal Dhaivata	$\underline{D}$	Minor Sixth	A flat
Shuddha Dhaivata	D	Major Sixth	A natural
Komal Nishada	$\underline{N}$	Minor Seventh	B flat
Shuddha Nishada	N	Major Seventh	B natural

In Western music, there are different symbols used to indicate notes of different lengths and there are symbols known as clefs which fix the pitch of the notes on the staff. These clef signs are placed at the beginning of the notes. The different clef signs used are as follows:

1) 

This is called the treble or G clef. It fixes the pitch of the second line from the bottom as G above middle C. Also, the second line of the staff goes through the middle of the circle of this clef.

2) 

This is called the bass or F clef. This fixes the pitch of the fourth line from the bottom as F below middle C. There are two dots on either side of the fourth line.

3) 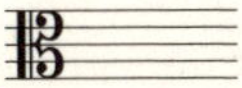

This is called the alto clef. This fixes the pitch of the third line as middle C.

4) 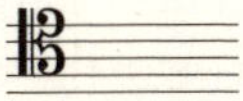

This is called the tenor clef. This fixes the fourth line from the bottom as middle C.

Both alto and tenor clefs are also known as C clefs. There is also a soprano clef where the same C clef symbol is placed on the bottom line of the staff, fixing this line as middle C. However, this is not in use any more.

Generally, in the Carnatic system, the diminished, minor, major and augmented notes are distinguished from one another by the numbers 1, 2 and 3 following the notes respectively. In the Hindustani system, the minor notes are distinguished from the major by a line below the note (—) except in the case of the fourth degree (M), where the augmented or sharp fourth is distinguished from the perfect fourth by a vertical line above the note (I).

Typically, when a composition is notated, the name of the raga on which it is based is written on the top or, in some cases, the ascending and descending notes of the scale are written in notation.

For example, in Raga Shankarabharanam (which is similar to the Western major scale), it is written as follows:

Raga Shankarabharanam	
Arohana (Ascending)	$S\ R_2\ G_3\ M_1\ P\ D_2\ N_3\ \dot{S}$
Avarohana (Descending)	$\dot{S}\ N_3\ D_2\ P\ M_1\ G_3\ R_2\ S$

Raga Shankarabharanam	
Ascending (Arohana)	$S\ R_2\ G_2\ M_1\ P\ D_2\ N_2\ \dot{S}$
In the Western scale	C D E F G A B C
	with C as tonic
Descending (Avarohana)	$\dot{S}\ N_2\ D_2\ P\ M_1\ G_2\ R_2\ S$
In the Western scale	C B A G F E D C

The Western clef sign is of no consequence in Indian music as the notation system indicates only the intervals between the notes without indicating any specific pitch. All the compositions in south Indian music can be played on any instrument such as the violin, veena, or flute, unlike in Western music where compositions are written for specific instruments or voice. Hence, any composition can be sung or played from any pitch that the performer chooses. For example, in Indian music a composition based on the major scale may be played or sung in A major, B major, C sharp major and so on, whereas in Western music a violin sonata in G major is always played in G major.

Though there are only seven notes in the octave (S, R, G, M, P, D, N), the music uses a much wider range of sounds than these seven notes, so the same notes are repeated again. Thus, when we reach S in the higher octave, we start over with R, G, M and so on. once again. Thus, the question arises, how does one distinguish between the two notes in different octaves? For this, we use a dot (.), either above or below the note. A dot above the note (Ṡ) indicates that the particular note is one octave higher than a note without a dot (S).

In other words, if C is tonic:

S 

Ṡ 

Similarly, a dot below the note (Ṣ) indicates that the note is an octave lower than the note without the dot (S).

In earlier days, since most of the compositions were vocal compositions, which generally covered less than three octaves, these dots sufficed to indicate these three octaves. But now, due to advancement in techniques of instruments like the violin, that allows them to span a much wider range, the old system is no longer adequate to indicate the extra range. Hence, I use my own system, which allows me to know whether a note is two or three octaves higher or lower. This is done by using the corresponding number before the dot. For example:

^{2}Ṡ indicates that it is two octaves higher than S;
^{3}Ṡ is three octaves higher than S, and so on.

Besides the dot, there are a few more symbols that are commonly used in the Carnatic notation system:

- (,) a comma after a note indicates an increase of one note value from the note it follows.
- (;) a semicolon indicates an increase of two note units from the note it follows.
- (|) a single vertical line indicates the end of a section of the tala.
- (‖) double vertical lines indicate the end of one rhythmic or tala cycle.
- (–) when a line is drawn below or above any notes, the notes must be played twice as fast as the other notes without the lines.

(=) double lines below or above the notes indicate that they be played twice as fast as notes with one line below or above. This also applies to the commas and semicolons which are used to extend the note value.

When a group of notes is played faster than the normal tempo, instead of using separate lines above or below the notes, we use one or two long lines depending on the speed as indicated above. So instead of S,, M P M G R we write S,,M PMGR (or S;M PMGR) connecting all the separate lines under each note to form one long line.

There is also another school of notation which uses capital and small letters. Notes written in capital letters are twice the value of notes in small letters. For example, S = s,.

In some schools of notation, there is no separate sign or symbol for silence or rest in the music. We use the same comma (,) or semicolon (;) to indicate the silence. For example, if a composition starts two pulses after the downbeat, or samam (the first beat of the tala cycle, where each beat is divided into four pulses), it is notated as follows:

,,NR GMPM GMGR S,,,‖ (or; NR GMPM GMGR S; ,‖)

Here, as mentioned earlier, the double line (‖) indicates the end of one cycle of tala, in this case, a four-beat cycle of the Eka tala (see chapter on Rhythmic Concepts for a detailed explanation of tala). Here, the semicolon not only indicates a two-pulse silence in the beginning of the melodic line, but also at the end, after the last note (S), along with the comma, it increases the value of the S to make it four pulses for the last beat, which implies that the last note is to be held till the end of the cycle. This is a major difference from the Western system where there are definite symbols (rests) used to indicate the length of the silence. Also, there are definite symbols used to indicate the length of the notes.

For example:

TABLE 3.5

Note Symbols	*American Names*	*English Names*	*Rest Symbols*
𝅜	Double Whole Note	Breve	𝄺
𝅝	Whole Note	Semibreve	𝄻
𝅗𝅥	Half Note	Minim	𝄼
𝅘𝅥	Quarter Note	Crotchet	𝄽
𝅘𝅥𝅮	Eighth Note	Quaver	𝄾
𝅘𝅥𝅯	Sixteenth Note	Semiquaver	𝄿

Let me point out some more differences that exist between the Western and Carnatic notation systems.

(1) The indication of the dynamics in the Western system where different signs are used, for example:

Piano (meaning soft) indicated by *p*
Mezzo piano (partly soft) indicated by *mp*
Pianissimo (very soft) indicated by *pp*
Forte (loud) indicated by *f*
Mezzo forte (partly loud) indicated by *mf*
Fortissimo (very loud) indicated by *ff*

In the Carnatic system, the dynamics are left to the imagination and interpretation of the artist.

(2) In Western music, compositions are written specifically for different instruments and, in order to cover different ranges of various instruments, different clef signs are used. In case of the keyboard and the harp, music is written using two clef signs (treble and bass clefs) on two staffs, to indicate the treble and bass notes, respectively, for the right and left hands and to cover the wide range. In Indian music, this is not needed since the notation system does not indicate any specific pitch; it only indicates the relative intervals. Besides, most compositions are vocal compositions, which are played on different instruments, hence the range is limited.

(3) In Indian music, the melodic concept, using microtones and ornamentations, is so advanced that one would have to create and use a great number of symbols to indicate the specific type of ornamentation and microtones in great detail. Also, since the interpretation of the same composition varies a great deal from one performer to the next, each performer would have to vary the notation to suit his/her needs. Sliding towards a note is a very common ornamentation. The same note could be approached from the note above, sliding down, or from the note below, sliding up, or sliding beyond the note and then coming back to it, either from below or above. The magnitude of the slide could also vary from person to person along with the speed of the slide and the number of repetitions.

In the figure shown, the dot indicates the note and the lines indicate some ways of approaching the note by sliding from notes above and below.

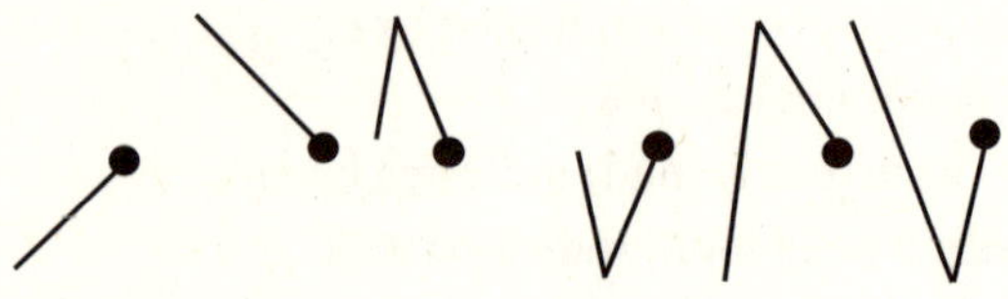

In Western music, ornamentations like trill, turn and tremolo have specific signs to indicate them and there is not much difference in interpretation of these ornamentations between different performers.

(4) In Western music, the tempo is indicated at the beginning of each movement in a composition by terms like adagio, allegro and andante, meaning slow, brisk and moderate, respectively (a movement is a section of a large composition like a concerto or sonata). It is common today to include metronome markings to indicate the number of beats per minute (for a specific note value). In Indian music, the tempo is left to the performer's discretion and, at times, the same composition could be sung or played from the extremely fast to the extremely slow tempo (or anywhere in between!) depending on the performer. And this is allowed and perfectly acceptable.

In orchestral compositions like symphonies and concertos and in chamber music compositions like sonatas and string quartets, there are always tempo changes with each movement. In Carnatic music, musical forms like varnam, kriti, padam or tillana are also divided into sections, but all played almost at the same tempo. However, at times, the performer may speed up the tempo of the last section (for example, the charanam section of the kriti) in order to create an impact.

(5) A dot following a note symbol increases the note value by one-half in the Western system, whereas in Indian music a comma increases the note value by an equal length and a semicolon increases it by two. The value of the rest (used for silence) is also increased by one-half when a dot follows the rest symbol in Western notation. In south Indian music, the comma and semicolon are also used to indicate a rest or silence as opposed to Western notation which has specific signs for rest. This is because once the composition starts in the Indian system there is no rest till the end of the section. The accompanying percussionists usually 'fill the gaps' with rhythmic patterns

between the sections and lead the main artist to the beginning of the next section. So there is no absolute silence once the composition starts. Silence is not part of the composition in Carnatic music, unlike in Western music. Hence, there is no need for the rest symbol, except at the beginning of the composition, if the composition starts after the downbeat. Typically, the vocal or melodic instruments leave a gap between the sections, while the percussionist is 'filling up'. The length of the rest between sections is not fixed since it depends on the improvisation of the percussionist. It could normally vary from half to two-and-a-half (or more) rhythmic cycles.

(6) In the case of music for instruments like the violin, in the West, there are indications for the bowing, like up-bow (V), or down-bow (Π). Often, the left hand fingerings are also marked, thus telling the performer exactly what to do. For other instruments, there can be similar specific indications. This is also done in orchestral scores for uniformity within sections of the different instruments. In south Indian music, there are no such indications as the compositions are written for the voice and there are no separate instrumental forms and notations. The instrumentalists usually adapt the compositions to suit their own style of playing.

(7) In Western music, a dot over the note is used to indicate that the note is to be played slightly shorter and detached (the term used is staccato) whereas in Indian music, a dot over the note indicates that it is to be played an octave higher.

(8) In the Western system, there are thirteen major scales (six with sharp key signatures, six with flat key signatures and one natural, C major, scale). Each major scale has a relative minor scale with the same key signature, starting a minor third below the corresponding major scale. There are three types of minor scales: (1) natural minor (2) harmonic minor and (3) melodic minor. In the natural minor, the third, sixth and seventh degrees are minor intervals and they are in both ascending and descending

scales. This corresponds to the twentieth mela, Natabhairavi. In the harmonic minor, the third and the sixth degrees are minor intervals, but the seventh degree is a major seventh in both ascending and descending scales. This corresponds to the twenty-first mela, Kiravani. In the melodic minor, the third degree is a minor third interval in both ascending and descending scales, but the sixth and seventh degrees are major sixth and major seventh in the ascending scale but a minor sixth and seventh in the descending scale. In addition, there are also chromatic scales made up of semitone intervals. In Carnatic music, Raga Shankarabharanam remains the same whether it is sung in C or C# or D, as long as the intervals between the notes remain the same. Seen from a Western classical perspective, in a particular key, there are seventy-two parent scales and from these there are millions of derived scales. For example, Raga Kiravani in C will be C minor (Harmonic) and the same Raga Kiravani in A will be A minor (Harmonic).

Another important difference is that in the Western system the above-mentioned scales are obtained by shifting the tonic, whereas in the Indian system the tonic is a constant factor and the scales are obtained by methodically changing the intervals between the seven notes in the octave (refer to the chapter on Melodic Concepts for details).

(9) Rhythmically, there is a complex system of 175 talas in the Carnatic system, in addition to the chapu talas and other groups of talas, as opposed to the Western system which has a handful of time signatures indicated by two numbers, one above the other. The upper number, or numerator, indicates the number of beats in a bar and the bottom number, or denominator, indicates the kind of notes the bar is divided into. Also, in the Carnatic system, when each beat is further subdivided into three, four, five, seven and nine pulses or their multiples (nadai), the division is strict and each of the subdivided notes is of equal length, not always the case in the West, since there is no concept of the nadai. For

example, when there is a group of notes of equal length against the beat or in a whole bar, the Western performer plays them freely and is not expected to strictly adhere to the equal length of the pulses. Also sometimes, towards the end, he may slow down, which is not allowed in the Indian system.

(10) Since spontaneous improvisation by the performer plays a major role in Indian classical music, notated music does not have much relevance here. In Western classical music, however, there is almost no improvisation. In ensemble playing, like a quartet or an orchestra, every member has his own notated parts to follow under the guidance of the leader, who, in the case of an orchestra, is the conductor. In Indian classical music, in ensemble playing, there is the main artist who is followed by melodic and rhythmic accompaniments. The accompanists listen, imitate and also improvise, in addition to playing the composed portions along with the main artist. In some cases, they just follow the main artist even without knowing the composition if the main artist decides to play a composition that they are not familiar with.

The notation system, as mentioned earlier, is merely a skeletal representation to jog the memory and is never used during a concert or even during practice, since the compositions are memorised when learning from the teacher. Even with a basic notation system, in actual performance the compositions rendered may vary a great deal from person to person. This is because of the spontaneous creative addition of melodic variations (known as sangatis) to the different melodic lines by the performer. These variations depend on the technical and musical ability of the performer.

4

Introduction to the Melodic Systems of Indian Classical Music

Since both Carnatic and Hindustani music were originally derived from the same source, there are many melodic similarities between the two.

As in other styles of music, in both classical styles, there are seven notes (see The Notation System).

Indian music is based on relative pitch. All notes are in relation to the tonic (Shadja), which can be any pitch. A performer can fix any note as the Shadja, and all other notes are named according to the intervals between them and the tonic note.

Sa is the tonic and can be any note. For female voices, Sa is commonly F#, G or G#, while for a male voice C or C# is more common.

In Indian classical music, it is normal for a musician to choose a particular pitch suitable to his/her voice or instrument and stay in that pitch for the whole concert. The tonic does not normally change for different compositions. In rare cases, a composition is sung or played in madhyama-shruti (shifting the tonic, Sa, to the position of the subdominant, Ma).

Indian classical music uses a tambura or a drone instrument. Since in Indian music, pitch is relative to the tonic, the drone is a constant reminder of the tonic. Each note is given a value only in relation to the tonic. For example, when we sing Ma it is given a place in relation to Sa. It is the fourth degree in relation to the tonic.

In a four-stringed drone instrument (tambura), the first string will usually be tuned to dominant (Pa), the second and third strings will be tuned to the tonic (Sa) above it, and the fourth string will be tuned to the tonic (Sa) below it. In some cases, the first string could be tuned to the subdominant (Ma) or even the leading note (Ni), depending on the raga. For example, while performing Raga Hindolam (Malkauns), the first string can be tuned to the subdominant (Ma) since the raga does not have a dominant (Pa).

Indian classical music uses the concept of ragas. A raga is a melodic concept based on a scale, which is similar to the concept of mode (in Western music). In order for a scale to be considered a raga, some notes (called Vadi and Samvadi swaras) are emphasised. The raga must incorporate ornamentation (called gamakas) and aesthetic elements, as laid out in the tradition. This gives a certain emotional colour, flavour and definite shape to the raga.

It is useful to note that melodically, in any raga the Sa is fixed. If the raga has a Pa, that is also fixed. There are no variations to Sa and Pa, while other notes are variable. In south Indian classical music, Ma has two variations while Ri, Ga, Da and Ni have three variations each. This system helps to create the seventy-two melakarta concept. North Indian classical music uses a different system where Ri, Ga, Ma, Da and Ni all have two variations each. In performing dhrupad, an entirely different system is followed.

HISTORICAL DEVELOPMENT OF THE RAGA SYSTEM

The evolution of the raga and mela (scale) concepts can be traced through lakshana-granthas (treatises about musical theory) that have been written on music over the centuries. Here is a brief overview of the different melodic concepts that predate the current melakarta system:

One of the earliest melodic classifications is the the grama-murcchana-jati system. Gramas are described as the group of swaras in an octave, just like a group of orderly houses in a village.

Bharata's *Natyashastra* states that murcchanas are scales (like present-day melas) and when the lakshanas (characteristics) are added they evolve into jatis (later called ragas).

Narada's *Sangita Makaranda* recognised jatis as full-fledged ragas and was the first to classify ragas in male and female forms (ragas and raginis), and the offspring form, putra ragas.

After the jatis, the next form to take shape in the evolution of the raga concept is the grama raga. Grama ragas are of two kinds: shuddha (pure) and vikrita (changed).

Matanga classified ragas as shuddha-chayalaga-sankeerna in his *Brihaddesi.* According to this classification, shuddha ragas are those which have 'pure notes', that is, notes that do not have traces of any other notes, with totally independent characteristics and raga bhava (emotion of the raga). This later paved the way for melakartas.

Chayalaga (also called saalaga or saalanka) refers to ragas that have a foreign note or borrow one or more notes from a different raga. These ragas occasionally have the tonality of another raga.

Sankeerna (also called mishra or sankrama) ragas have tonalities of more than two ragas.

Parsvadeva in *Sangita Samayasara* classifies ragas as raaganga (with notes belonging only to a given raga), upanga (by omitting certain notes), bhashanga (with foreign notes) and kriyanga (used for specific rituals). By combining each of these with sampoorna (with seven notes), shadava (with six notes) and audava (with five notes) he presented twelve sets of ragas, such as, raaganga sampoorna, upanga audava and so on.

In Narada's *Sangita Makaranda*, there emerged the classification of ragas based on various factors: purusha (masculine), stree (feminine) and napumsaka (neutral) ragas; raga (male), ragini (female) and their putra (child); muktanga kampita, ardha kampita and kampaviheena, on the basis of gamakas (ornamentation); and early morning, morning, afternoon, evening, and night ragas based on when the raga should be sung or played.

In the marga (classical) and deshi (folk) raga classification, marga ragas are those that were born from jatis and strictly adhered to rules, while deshi ragas are those that underwent changes over the years. Only some rules from marga ragas were followed in deshi ragas.

Ramamatya, in the *Swaramelakalanidhi* referred to uttama-madhyama-adhama. This was followed by Somanatha in his *Raga Vibodha*. Shuddha ragas, which had independent characteristics without taking the shades of any other ragas, were called uttama ragas. These ragas were believed to be ideal for detailed elaboration of ragas and taanas and appropriate for composing. They were very popular ragas. Madhyama ragas were basic in their characteristics and very few types of compositions could be composed in them. These ragas were rare. Adhama ragas were not suitable for scholarly compositions.

EVOLUTION OF THE MELAS

Vidyaranya was the first to use the term 'mela' to denote a parent raga. Classification of ragas in Carnatic music began with the scheme of mela (parent) and janya (derived) ragas. Vidyaranya developed a system of fifteen melas, and they were named as follows: Natta, Gurjari, Varatika, Sriraga, Bhairavi, Shankarabharana, Ahiri, Vasantabhairavi, Samanta, Kambodhi, Mukhari, Shuddharamakriya, Kedaragowla, Hejjujji and Deshakshi.

He also dealt with fifty derived ragas. It is interesting to note that the order of these melas is not in any logical sequence.

Ramamatya's *Swaramelakalanidhi* was based on Sarangadeva's

Sangita Ratnakara, and was published in 1550. This was the first work to use the word 'mela' in its title. Ramamatya proposed five vikrita (changeable) swaras, for a total of twelve swaras in an octave (that is, Ri, Ga, Ma, Da and Ni). Ramamatya is known as the 'father of the mela concept', as he was the first to devote a separate chapter on mela, known as 'Melaprakarana'. He provides a list of twenty melas and sixty-four janya ragas, where Shadja and Panchama are fixed notes.

Raga Vibodha was inspired by *Swaramelakalanidhi,* but was far more advanced in the aspects of swara, shruti, mela and raga.

Sangita Sudha is a seventeenth-century work by Govinda Dikshitar, which presents an in-depth discussion on the styles and systems of music present at the time of its being written. It discusses two hundred and sixty-four ragas, and the lakshanas for about fifty. This work also provides insight into the *Sangeetasaara* of Vidyaranya.

Venkatamakhi's seminal work, the *Chaturdandiprakashika,* written in 1650, had a profound influence on every musician that came after. Venkatamakhi laid the foundation for the seventy-two mela system, but only described nineteen of them. The names for all of them were given by his grandson, Muddu Venkatamakhi, who also composed lakshana-gitas in each, and published them in his work *Ragalakshanam.*

The melakarta concept uses the twelve semitones, enharmonically divided into sixteen notes. (See The Notation System.)

Bhutasankhya

Around the time of the publication of Venkatamakhi's work, the Bhutasankhya system was popular among mathematicians and astronomers. This was the concept of using Sanskrit words to denote the numerical values associated with them. This system was used to name the chakras (groups of melakarta ragas; each chakra has six ragas and there are a total of twelve chakras) as follows:

TABLE 4.1
Bhutasankhya

Chakra	*Name*	*Meaning*		*Details*
I	Indu	1	Moon	
II	Netra	2	Eyes	
III	Agni	3	Types of fire	Dakshina, Aavaahaneeya, Garhapathya
IV	Veda	4	Vedas	Rig, Yajur, Sama, Atharva
V	Baana	5	Arrows of Manmatha	Lotus, Mango, Ashoka, Jasmine and Blue Water Lily flowers
VI	Ritu	6	Seasons	Vasanta, Greeshma, Varsha, Sharad, Hemanta and Shishira
VII	Rishi	7	Sages	Atri, Bhrigu, Bharadwaja, Vishwamitra, Vasishta, Gautama and Kashyapa (Different texts give different lists)
VIII	Vasu	8	Elemental deities	Dhara (Earth), Anala (Fire), Apa (Water), Anila (Wind), Dhruva (North Star), Some (Moon), Prabhasa (Dawn) and Pratyusha (Light)

Chakra	Name	Meaning		Details
IX	Brahma	9	Prajapatis (deities presiding over protection of lives)	Angiras, Atri, Kashyapa, Pulastya, Pulaha, Bhrigu, Marichi, Vasishta and Daksha
X	Dishi	10	Directions	Uttara (north), Dakshina (south), Purva (east), Paschima (west), Agneya (south-east), Nairutya (south-west), Vayavya (north-west), Eeshanya (north-east), Akasha (sky), Bhumi (earth)
XI	Rudra	11	Deities presiding over dissolution	Mahadeva, Shiva, Rudra, Shankara, Nilalohita, Ishana, Vijaya, Bhima, Devadeva, Bhava, Kapali
XII	Aditya	12	Deities of preservation	Amsha, Aryaman, Bhaga, Daksha, Mitra, Pusan, Sakra, Savitr, Tvastar, Varuna, Vishnu, Vivasvat

Katapayadi Sutra

The Katapayadi system was first seen in 683 CE, in Haridatta's *Graha-chara-nibandhana*. The system was based on substituting letters for numerals to make them memorable, and has been applied to both the asampurna and sampurna mela systems, as well as to suladi talas.

Numbers correspond to sounds in the following way:

TABLE 4.2
Katapayadi Sutra

Number	*Sounds*
1	ka, ta, pa, ya
2	kha, tta, pha, ra
3	ga, da, ba, la
4	gha, dha, bha, va
5	na, nna, ma, sha
6	cha, tha, ssha
7	chha, thha, sa
8	ja, da, ha
9	jha, ddha,
0	nna, na

By taking the corresponding numbers of the first two consonants of a raga name, and reversing those numbers, one can derive the mela number. For example, if we take the name Kanakambari, the first two consonants are 'ka' and 'na': if we reverse it, we get 'na' (corresponding to 0) and 'ka' (corresponding to 1), which gives us 01, the number of the melakarta.

The seventy-two ragas according to this asampurna mela paddhati are as follows (Sundaram Iyer):

TABLE 4.3
Seventy-two ragas according to Asampurna Mela Paddhati

Chakra Name	*Scale*	*Ascending*	*Descending*	*Asampurna Mela*
I Indu	1	$S R_1 M_1 P D_1 S$	$S N_1 D_1 P M_1 G_1 R_1 S$	Kanakambari
	2	$S R_1 M_1 P D_1 P N_2 S$	$S N_2 D_1 P M_1 G_1 R_1 S$	Phenadhyuti
	3	$S R_1 M_1 P D_1 N_3 S$	$S N_3 D_1 P M_1 G_1 R_1 S$	Ganasamavarali
	4	$S R_1 M_1 P D_2 N_2 S$	$S N_2 D_2 P M_1 G_1 R_1 S$	Bhanumati
	5	$S R_1 M_1 P D_2 N_3 S$	$S N_3 D_2 P M_1 G_1 R_1 S$	Manoranjani
	6	$S R_1 M_1 P N_3 S$	$S N_3 D_2 N_3 P M_1 G_1 R_1 S$	Tanukirthi
II Netra	7	$S R_1 G_2 R_1 M_1 G_2 M_1 P N_1 D_1 S$	$S N_1 D_1 P M_1 G_2 M_1 G_2 R_1 S$	Senagrini
	8	$S R_1 G_2 M_1 P D_1 N_2 S$	$S N_2 D_1 M_1 P G_2 R_1 S$	Janatodi
	9	$S R_1 G_2 M_1 P D_1 N_3 S$	$S N_3 D_1 P M_1 G_2 R_1 S$	Dhunibhinnashadjam
	10	$S G_2 M_1 P N_2 D_2 N_2 S$	$S N_2 D_2 N_2 P N_2 P M_1 G_2 G_2 R_1 R_1 S$	Natabharanam
	11	$S R_1 G_2 M_1 P D_2 N_3 S$	$S N_3 D_2 P M_1 G_2 R_1 S$	Kokilaravam
	12	$S R_1 M_1 P S$	$S N_3 D_3 N_3 P M_1 G_2 S$	Rupavati
III Agni	13	$S R_1 M_1 G_3 M_1 P D_1 S$	$S N_1 D_1 P M_1 G_3 R_1 S$	Geyahejjajji
	14	$S R_1 G_3 M_1 P D_1 N_2 S$	$S N_2 D_1 M_1 G_3 M_1 P M_1 G_3 R_1 S$	Vadivasantabhairavi
	15	$S R_1 G_3 M_1 P D_1 N_3 S$	$S N_3 D_1 P M_1 G_3 R_1 S$	Mayamalavagaula

Chakra Name	*Scale*	*Ascending*	*Descending*	*Asampurna Mela*
	16	$S R_1 G_3 M_1 P D_2 N_2 S$	$S N_2 D_2 P M_1 G_3 R_1 S$	Thoyavegavahini
	17	$S R_1 G_3 M_1 D_2 N_3 S$	$S N_3 D_2 P M_1 G_3 R_1 S$	Chayavati
	18	$S R_1 G_3 M_1 P N_3 S$	$S N_3 D_3 N_3 P M_1 G_3 R_1 S$	Jayashuddhamalavi
IV Veda	19	$S R_2 G_2 M_1 P D_1 N_1 D_1 P D_1 S$	$S N_1 D_1 P M_1 G_2 R_2 G_2 R_2 S$	Jhankarabhramari
	20	$S G_2 R_2 G_2 M_1 N_2 D_1 M_1 N_2 N_2 S$	$S N_2 D_1 M_1 G_2 M_1 P M_1 G_2 R_2 S$	Nariritigowla
	21	$S R_2 M_1 P D_1 P D_1 N_3 S$	$S N_3 P D_1 P M_1 P G_2 R_2 S$	Kiranavali
	22	$S R_2 M_1 P N_2 S$	$S N_2 P D_2 N_2 P M_1 R_2 G_2 R_2 S$	Shree
	23	$S R_2 G_2 S R_2 M_1 P D_2 S$	$S N_3 D_2 P M_1 G_2 R_2 S$	Gourivelavali
	24	$S R_2 M_1 P N_3 D_3 N_3 S$	$S N_3 P M_1 M_1 R_2 G_2 S$	Veeravasantam
V Baana	25	$S M_1 G_3 M_1 P D_1 N_1 D_1 S$	$S N_1 D_1 P M_1 G_3 R_2 S$	Sharavati
	26	$S R_2 G_3 P D_1 N_2 D_1 P D_1 S$	$S D_1 P G_3 R_2 S R_2 G_3 M_1 G_3 R_2 S$	Tarangini
	27	$S R_2 G_3 M_1 P D_1 N_3 S$	$S N_3 D_1 P M_1 G_3 R_2 G_3 S$	Sowrasena
	28	$S R_2 G_3 M_1 P D_2 N_2 S$	$S N_2 D_2 P M_1 G_3 R_2 S$	Harikedaragowla
	29	$S R_2 G_3 M_1 P D_2 N_3 S$	$S N_3 D_2 P M_1 G_3 R_2 S$	Dhirasankarabharanam
	30	$S R_2 G_3 M_1 P N_3 D_3 N_3 S$	$S N_3 P M_1 G_3 R_2 S$	Nagabharanam
VI Ritu	31	$S R_3 G_3 M_1 P D_1 N_1 P D_1 S$	$S N_1 D_1 P M_1 R_3 G_3 M_1 R_3 S$	Kalavati
	32	$S M_1 R_3 G_3 M_1 P N_2 N_2 S$	$S N_2 D_1 P M_1 M_1 R_3 S$	Ragachudamani

Chakra Name	*Scale*	*Ascending*	*Descending*	*Asampurna Mela*
	33	$S\,R_3\,G_3\,M_1\,P\,D_1\,N_3\,S$	$S\,N_3\,P\,D_1\,M_1\,M_1\,G_3\,M_1\,R_3\,S$	Gangatarangini
	34	$S\,R_3\,G_3\,M_1\,P\,N_2\,N_2\,S$	$S\,N_2\,D_2\,N_2\,P\,S\,N_2\,P\,M_1\,R_3\,S$	Bhogachayanata
	35	$S\,M_1\,G_3\,P\,D_2\,S$	$S\,N_3\,D_2\,S\,N_3\,P\,M_1\,R_3\,S$	Shailadeshakshi
	36	$S\,R_3\,G_3\,M_1\,P\,D_3\,N_3\,S$	$S\,N_3\,P\,M_1\,R_3\,S$	Chalanata
VII Rishi	37	$S\,G_1\,R_1\,G_1\,M_2\,P\,D_1\,S$	$S\,N_1\,D_1\,P\,M_2\,G_1\,R_1\,S$	Sowgandhini
	38	$S\,G_1\,R_1\,G_1\,M_2\,P\,D_1\,N_2\,S$	$S\,N_2\,D_1\,P\,M_2\,G_1\,R_1\,S$	Jaganmohanam
	39	$S\,G_1\,R_1\,G_1\,M_2\,P\,D_1\,N_3\,S$	$S\,N_3\,D_1\,P\,M_2\,G_1\,R_1\,S$	Dhalivarali
	40	$S\,G_1\,R_1\,G_1\,M_2\,P\,D_2\,P\,N_2\,S$	$S\,N_2\,D_2\,P\,M_2\,G_1\,R_1\,S$	Nabhamani
	41	$S\,G_1\,R_1\,G_1\,M_2\,P\,N_3\,D_2\,N_3\,S$	$S\,N_3\,D_2\,P\,M_2\,G_1\,R_1\,S$	Kumbhini
	42	$S\,G_1\,R_1\,G_1\,M_2\,P\,N_3\,D_3\,N_3\,S$	$S\,N_3\,P\,M_2\,G_1\,R_1\,S$	Ravikriya
VIII Vasu	43	$S\,R_1\,G_2\,M_2\,P\,D_1\,N1\,D_1\,P\,D_1\,S$	$S\,N_1\,D_1\,P\,M_2\,G_2\,R_1\,S$	Girvani
	44	$S\,R_1\,G_2\,M_2\,P\,D_1\,P\,N_2\,S$	$S\,N_2\,D_1\,P\,M_2\,G_2\,R_1\,S$	Bhavani
	45	$S\,R_1\,G_2\,M_2\,P\,D_1\,N_3\,S$	$S\,N_2\,D_2\,P\,M_2\,G_2\,R_1\,S$	Shivapantuvarali
	46	$S\,R_1\,M_2\,P\,D_2\,S$	$S\,N_2\,D_2\,P\,M_2\,G_2\,S$	Sthavarajam
	47	$S\,R_1\,G_2\,M_2\,P\,D_2\,N_3\,S$	$S\,N_3\,D_2\,M_2\,G_2\,R_1\,S$	Sowveeram
	48	$S\,R_1\,G_2\,M_2\,P\,D_3\,N_3\,S$	$S\,N_3\,P\,M_2\,G_2\,R_1\,S$	Jeevantika

Chakra Name	Scale	Ascending	Descending	Asampurna Mela
IX Brahma	49	$S R_1 G_3 M_2 P D_1 S$	$S N_1 D_1 P M_2 G_3 R_1 S$	Dhavalangam
	50	$S R_1 G_3 M_2 P D_1 N_2 S$	$S N_2 D_1 P M_2 G_3 R_1 S$	Namadeshi
	51	$S G_3 R_1 G_3 M_2 P D_1 N_3 S$	$S N_3 D_1 P M_2 G_3 R_1 S$	Kashiramakriya
	52	$S R_1 G_3 M_2 P D_2 N_2 S$	$S N_2 D_2 P M_2 G_3 R_1 S$	Ramamanohari
	53	$S R_1 G_3 M_2 P D_2 P S$	$S N_3 D_2 P M_2 G_3 R_1 S$	Gamakakriya
	54	$S R_1 G_3 M_2 P D_3 N_3 S$	$S N_3 P M_2 G_3 R_1 S$	Vamshavati
X Disi	55	$S R_2 G_2 M_2 P D_1 S$	$S N_1 D_1 P M_2 G_2 R_2 S$	Shamalam
	56	$S R_2 G_2 M_2 P D_1 N_2 S$	$S N_2 D_1 P M_2 G_2 R_2 S$	Chamaram
	57	$S R_2 G_2 M_2 P D_1 N_3 S$	$S N_3 D_1 P M_2 G_2 R_2 S$	Sumadhyuti
	58	$S R_2 G_2 M_2 P D_2 N_2 S$	$S N_2 D_2 P M_2 G_2 R_2 S$	Deshisimharavam
	59	$S R_2 G_2 M_2 P D_2 N_3 S$	$S N_3 D_2 P M_2 G_2 R_2 S$	Dhaamavati
	60	$S R_2 G_2 M_2 P D_3 N_3 S$	$S N_3 P M_2 G_2 R_2 S$	Nishadam
XI Rudra	61	$S R_2 G_3 M_2 P D_1 S$	$S N_1 D_1 P M_2 G_3 R_2 S$	Kuntalam
	62	$S R_2 G_3 M_2 P D_1 N_2 S$	$S N_2 D_1 P M_2 G_3 R_2 S$	Ratipriya
	63	$S R_2 G_3 M_2 P D_1 N_3 S$	$S N_3 D_1 P M_2 G_3 R_2 S$	Geetapriya
	64	$S R_2 G_3 M_2 P D_2 N_2 S$	$S N_2 D_2 P M_2 G_3 R_2 S$	Bhushavati

Chakra Name	*Scale*	*Ascending*	*Descending*	*Asampurna Mela*
	65	$S R_2 G_3 M_2 P D_2 N_3 S$	$S N_3 D_2 P M_2 G_3 R_2 S$	Shantakalyani
	66	$S R_2 G_3 M_2 P D_3 N_3 S$	$S N_3 P M_2 G_3 R_2 S$	Chaturangini
XII Aditya	67	$S R_3 G_3 M_2 P D_1 S$	$S N_1 D_1 P M_2 R_3 S$	Santamanjari
	68	$S R_3 G_3 M_2 P D_1 N_2 S$	$S N_2 D_1 P M_2 G_3 S$	Jyoti
	69	$S R_3 G_3 M_2 P D_1 N_3 S$	$S N_3 D_1 P M_2 R_3 G_3 S$	Dhowtapanchamam
	70	$S R_3 G_3 M_2 P D_2 N_3 S$	$S N_2 D_2 P M_2 R_3 G_3 S$	Nasamani
	71	$S R_3 G_3 M_2 P D_2 N_3 S$	$S N_3 D_2 P M_2 R_3 G_3 S$	Kusumakaram
	72	S R3 G3 S P M2 P $N_3 D_3 N_3 S$	$S N_3 D_3 N_3 P M_2 P R_3 G_3 S$	Rasamanjari

Venkatamakhi's classification inspired many other scholars, including Hindustani musicologist V.N. Bhatkhande who wanted 'rules of ragas to be fixed in north Indian music in a manner that they were fixed in south Indian music' and believed *Chaturdandi Prakasika* would be 'central to the effort of restoring order to the then disordered state of Hindustani music'.

Srinivasa's *Raga Tattva Vibodha* and Ahobala's *Sangita Parijata* (both seventeenth century texts) highlight the classification of melas.

MODERN CARNATIC RAGA SYSTEM

The present Carnatic melodic system is based on Govindacharya's melakarta concept, with seventy-two melakarta or janaka scales and millions of janya scales.

The characteristics of melakarta ragas are:

1. The raga must contain all the seven notes: Sa, Ri, Ga, Ma, Pa, Da and Ni. For example, in the melakarta raga Shankarabharanam, the notes are Sa Ri_2 Ga_3 Ma_1 Pa Da_2 Ni_3.
2. The notes must be in sequence. For example, we cannot have Sa Ga Ri Ma Pa Da Ni **Sa** in the arohana.
3. They must be the same in the arohana and avarohana. For example, in Shankarabharanam, the notes in the avarohana are **Sa** Ni_3 Da_2 Pa Ma_1 Ga_3 Ri_2 Sa.
4. There are no other (foreign) notes in the scale. For example, in Shankarabharanam, we cannot include Ri_1 or Ma_2 because they are foreign notes to this particular melakarta.

Of the seventy-two melakartas, the first thirty-six are very similar to the second thirty-six with the only difference being that the first thirty-six use a perfect fourth (shuddha madhyama) and the second thirty-six use an augmented fourth (prati madhyama).

Each group of thirty-six ragas is further divided into groups of six known as chakras. In each chakra, the first tetrachord is the same, and the second tetrachord changes by one note.

TABLE 4.4
Melakarta Ragas

Chakra Name		*Ascending*								*Mela*
I Indu	1	S	R_1	G_1	M_1	P	D_1	N_1	S	Kanakangi
	2	S	R_1	G_1	M_1	P	D_1	N_2	S	Ratnangi
	3	S	R_1	G_1	M_1	P	D_1	N_3	S	Ganamurti
	4	S	R_1	G_1	M_1	P	D_2	N_2	S	Vanaspati
	5	S	R_1	G_1	M_1	P	D_2	N_3	S	Manavati
	6	S	R_1	G_1	M_1	P	D_3	N_3	S	Tanarupi
II Netra	7	S	R_1	G_2	M_1	P	D_1	N_1	S	Senavati
	8	S	R_1	G_2	M_1	P	D_1	N_2	S	Hanumatodi
	9	S	R_1	G_2	M_1	P	D_1	N_3	S	Dhenuka
	10	S	R_1	G_2	M_1	P	D_2	N_2	S	Natakapriya
	11	S	R_1	G_2	M_1	P	D_2	N_3	S	Kokilapriya
	12	S	R_1	G_2	M_1	P	D_3	N_3	S	Rupavati
III Agni	13	S	R_1	G_3	M_1	P	D_1	N_1	S	Gayakapriya
	14	S	R_1	G_3	M_1	P	D_1	N_2	S	Vakulabharanam
	15	S	R_1	G_3	M_1	P	D_1	N_3	S	Mayamalavagaula
	16	S	R_1	G_3	M_1	P	D_2	N_2	S	Chakravakam
	17	S	R_1	G_3	M_1	P	D_2	N_3	S	Suryakantam
	18	S	R_1	G_3	M_1	P	D_3	N_3	S	Hatakambari
IV Veda	19	S	R_2	G_2	M_1	P	D_1	N_1	S	Jhankaradhvani
	20	S	R_2	G_2	M_1	P	D_1	N_2	S	Natabhairavi
	21	S	R_2	G_2	M_1	P	D_1	N_3	S	Kiravani
	22	S	R_2	G_2	M_1	P	D_2	N_2	S	Kharaharapriya
	23	S	R_2	G_2	M_1	P	D_2	N_3	S	Gourimanohari
	24	S	R_2	G_2	M_1	P	D_3	N_3	S	Varunapriya

Chakra Name		*Ascending*								*Mela*
V Bana	25	S	R_2	G_3	M_1	P	D_1	N_1	S	Mararanjani
	26	S	R_2	G_3	M_1	P	D_1	N_2	S	Charukesi
	27	S	R_2	G_3	M_1	P	D_1	N_3	S	Sarasangi
	28	S	R_2	G_3	M_1	P	D_2	N_2	S	Harikambhoji
	29	S	R_2	G_3	M_1	P	D_2	N_3	S	Dhirasankara-bharanam
	30	S	R_2	G_3	M_1	P	D_3	N_3	S	Naganandini
VI Ritu	31	S	R_3	G_3	M_1	P	D_1	N_1	S	Yagapriya
	32	S	R_3	G_3	M_1	P	D_1	N_2	S	Ragavardhani
	33	S	R_3	G_3	M_1	P	D_1	N_3	S	Gangeyabhushani
	34	S	R_3	G_3	M_1	P	D_2	N_2	S	Vagadhisvari
	35	S	R_3	G_3	M_1	P	D_2	N_3	S	Sulini
	36	S	R_3	G_3	M_1	P	D_3	N_3	S	Chalanata
VII Rishi	37	S	R_1	G_1	M_2	P	D_1	N_1	S	Salagam
	38	S	R_1	G_1	M_2	P	D_1	N_2	S	Jalarnavam
	39	S	R_1	G_1	M_2	P	D_1	N_3	S	Jhalavarali
	40	S	R_1	G_1	M_2	P	D_2	N_2	S	Navanitam
	41	S	R_1	G_1	M_2	P	D_2	N_3	S	Pavani
	42	S	R_1	G_1	M_2	P	D_3	N_3	S	Raghupriya
VIII Vasu	43	S	R_1	G_2	M_2	P	D_1	N_1	S	Gavambhodi
	44	S	R_1	G_2	M_2	P	D_1	N_2	S	Bhavapriya
	45	S	R_1	G_2	M_2	P	D_1	N_3	S	Subhapantuvarali
	46	S	R_1	G_2	M_2	P	D_2	N_2	S	Shadvidhamargini
	47	S	R_1	G_2	M_2	P	D_2	N_3	S	Suvarnangi
	48	S	R_1	G_2	M_2	P	D_3	N_3	S	Divyamani

Chakra Name		*Ascending*								*Mela*
IX Brahma	49	S	R_1	G_3	M_2	P	D_1	N_1	S	Dhavalambari
	50	S	R_1	G_3	M_2	P	D_1	N_2	S	Namanarayani
	51	S	R_1	G_3	M_2	P	D_1	N_3	S	Kamavardhini
	52	S	R_1	G_3	M_2	P	D_2	N_2	S	Ramapriya
	53	S	R_1	G_3	M_2	P	D_2	N_3	S	Gamanasrama
	54	S	R_1	G_3	M_2	P	D_3	N_3	S	Vishvambari
X Disi	55	S	R_2	G_2	M_2	P	D_1	N_1	S	Syamalangi
	56	S	R_2	G_2	M_2	P	D_1	N_2	S	Shanmukhapriya
	57	S	R_2	G_2	M_2	P	D_1	N_3	S	Simhendra-Madhyamam
	58	S	R_2	G_2	M_2	P	D_2	N_2	S	Hemavati
	59	S	R_2	G_2	M_2	P	D_2	N_3	S	Dharmavati
	60	S	R_2	G_2	M_2	P	D_3	N_3	S	Nitimati
XI Rudra	61	S	R_2	G_3	M_2	P	D_1	N_1	S	Kantamani
	62	S	R_2	G_3	M_2	P	D_1	N_2	S	Rishabhapriya
	63	S	R_2	G_3	M_2	P	D_1	N_3	S	Latangi
	64	S	R_2	G_3	M_2	P	D_2	N_2	S	Vachaspati
	65	S	R_2	G_3	M_2	P	D_2	N_3	S	Mechakalyani
	66	S	R_2	G_3	M_2	P	D_3	N_3	S	Chitrambari
XII Aditya	67	S	R_3	G_3	M_2	P	D_1	N_1	S	Sucharitra
	68	S	R_3	G_3	M_2	P	D_1	N_2	S	Jyotisvarupini
	69	S	R_3	G_3	M_2	P	D_1	N_3	S	Dhatuvardhani
	70	S	R_3	G_3	M_2	P	D_2	N_2	S	Nasikabhushani
	71	S	R_3	G_3	M_2	P	D_2	N_3	S	Kosalam
	72	S	R_3	G_3	M_2	P	D_3	N_3	S	Rasikapriya

DERIVED RAGAS

From these mela or janaka ragas, millions of janya ragas can be derived. There are four main ways of deriving ragas:

1. By omitting one or more notes (varjya ragas)
2. By rearranging the order of the notes (vakra ragas)
3. By adding a foreign note (bhashanga ragas)
4. By a combination of two or all of the above

These additions or omissions can be only in the ascending (Type 1), only in the descending (Type 2), or both (Type 3).

Ragas with five notes are known as audava, those with six notes are called shadava and ragas with seven notes are known as sampurna.

For example, if a raga has five notes in the ascending and descending, it is called an audava-audava raga; if a raga has six notes in the ascending and seven notes in the descending, it is called a shadava-sampurna raga, and so on.

THE DIFFERENCE BETWEEN A SCALE AND A RAGA

Ragas are based on scales, but just playing a scale up and down doesn't make it a raga. In a raga there is emphasis on certain primary notes, the vadi being the most significant note and the samvadi the second most important. The vadi is in the first half of the scale (purva anga) and the samvadi is in the second half (uttara anga). The samvadi is said to emphasise the importance of the vadi. The remaining notes are known as anuvadi or residual notes. The notes which are dissonant, and do not belong to the raga, are known as vivadi.

In addition to this, there are ornamentations (gamakas) that are essential to bring out the colour, flavour and the emotion of the raga. In many ragas, a key phrase that consists of a few notes with ornamentation, typically including the vadi or samvadi swaras, can make the connoisseur immediately recognise the raga.

Another characteristic feature of Carnatic music is its use of microtones, which are often less than a quartertone. Instead of dividing an octave into twelve semitones like in the West, an octave is divided into twenty-two shrutis (tones). Based on this system, the tonic and dominant are always fixed and can be only one tone each. The rest five of the seven notes (the supertonic or Ri, mediant or Ga, subdominant or Ma, submediant or Da, and the leading note or Ni) can each be of four types. Thus, there are twenty-two shrutis.

WHAT MAKES A SCALE A RAGA

In a raga, the different types of notes are:

1. Vadi: The swara which plays the most important part.
2. Samvadi: Any two swaras which are at an interval of nine or thirteen shrutis from each other and are mutually consonant. The interval between the vadi and samvadi is typically the same as that between the tonic and subdominant or tonic and dominant.
3. Vivadi: If the notes are at an interval of two shrutis and the swara sounds discordant to another then it is called vivadi.
4. Anuvadi: The remaining notes after vadi, samvadi and vivadi are the assonant notes called anuvadi.

Vadi and samvadi are the primary notes, which are emphasised during raga development. Usually the fourth or fifth note from the vadi is the samvadi.

These notes can be emphasised in different ways:

1. By repeating the note more frequently than other notes
2. By holding the notes for a longer duration than other notes
3. By keeping the note as the tonal centre, developing around it and coming back to that note as a resting note

In ragas, certain notes are ornamented with slides, known as gamakas. In certain cases, for the same note, multiple slides are used.

It is also common to slide towards a note, from a note below or from a note above, and it is even possible to slide more than one note interval, and in different directions to reach a note, in order to bring in the essence of the raga.

These will give a particular colour and mood to the raga.

In the figure shown, the dot indicates the note and the lines indicate some ways of approaching the note by sliding from notes above and below.

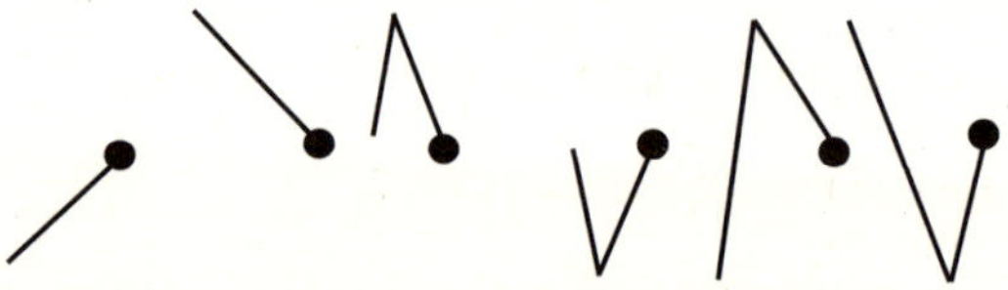

HINDUSTANI RAGA SYSTEM

The Hindustani melodic system is based on twelve notes.

The Hindustani raga system is based on ten parent scales known as thaats. From these scales, many others may be derived.

Since we have already learnt about the melakarta concept, it will be easier to connect the thaats to the melas:

Kalyan:	Mechakalyani
Bilawal:	Dheerashankarabharanam
Asavari:	Natabhairavi
Marwa:	Gamanashrama
Todi:	Shubhapantuvarali
Khamaj:	Harikambhoji
Bhairav:	Mayamalavagaula
Kafi:	Kharaharapriya
Poorvi:	Kamavardhini (Pantuvarali)
Bhairavi:	Hanumatodi

The janya scales in the Hindustani raga system come under one of these ten thaats. For example:

Kalyan Thaat:	Yaman, Bhupali, Hindol, Kedar, Kamod
Bilawal Thaat:	Deshkar, Hamsadhwani, Bihag
Asavari Thaat:	Asavari, Desi, Darbari, Adana, Jaunpuri
Marwa Thaat:	Marwa, Puriya, Bhatiyar, Bibhas, Sohini
Todi Thaat:	Miyan ki Todi, Gujari Todi, Madhuvanti, Multani
Khamaj Thaat:	Rageshree, Jhinjhoti, Desh, Tilang, Tilak Kamod, Jaijaiwanti, Kalavati
Bhairav Thaat:	Ramkali, Gunkali, Jogiya, Basant Mukhari, Bhairav
Kafi Thaat:	Dhanashree, Dhani, Bahar, Bhimpalasi, Pilu, Megh Malhar, Bageshree
Poorvi Thaat:	Puriya Dhanashree, Gauri, Shree, Paraj, Basant
Bhairavi Thaat:	Malkauns, Bilaskhani Todi, Bhupali Todi, Kaunsi Kanada

GHARANAS OF HINDUSTANI CLASSICAL MUSIC

In South Indian tradition, there are different 'banis'—where some great composers have created their own style of performing (which highlights their unique skills). Some banis have a more virtuosic approach, depending on the style of that particular singer or instrumentalist. Some others have more musical emphasis and ornamentation, which has given rise to different banis. Accordingly, we have different banis like Nagaswaram bani, Semmangudi bani, D. K. Pattammal bani, Madurai Mani Iyer bani, to name a few.

Similarly, in North Indian music there are great artists who have created different gharanas.

In north Indian or Hindustani classical music, the form of presentation typically varies from one gharana (family) to another. Gharanas became popular in the nineteenth century when musicians slowly began to lose royal patronage. Musicians moved to urban areas and to hold on to their identity, took refuge in the names of the regions they came from.

The term 'gharana' is derived from the Hindi word 'ghar, 'which is in turn derived from the Sanskrit word 'griha,' which means 'family' or 'house.' Therefore, even today, the names of many gharanas refer to places. Famous Khyal gharanas include those from Agra, Bhendibazaar, Gwalior, Indore, Jaipur, Kirana, Mewati, Patiala, and Rampur-Sahaswan.

According to Krishan Rao Pandit, 'A tradition of centuries, the intellect of gurus, and generations of guru shishya parampara all of these together make a gharana.' Gharana, in Hindustani music, stands for 'a community of performers who share a distinctive musical style that traces back to a particular instructor or region.' A 'distinctive musical style' in Hindustani tradition includes not only uniqueness of performance, but also a broader ideology of music, aesthetics and pedagogy. And that singing style must have been handed down to at least three generations before it may be deemed a gharana.

A gharana is generally started by a talented and creative musician who has created and developed a novel presentation for the raga and has further passed down the teaching to his disciples. When this process keeps going on for at least three generations a gharana is formed.

A creative musician develops his or her own unique style of presenting classical music. Over a period of time, this style crystallises into a form that connoisseurs can recognise and distinguish from other existing styles. This is then further passed on to the next generation of disciples by the musician, thus creating a tradition. In due course, that unique style of singing acquires an appellation, typically named after the place of origin of the pioneering musician. This is how a gharana gets formed.

A musical presentation which is backed by a long tradition and is marked by discipline, methodology and neatness is known as gharana. In relation to music, gharana refers to a family of musicians, a school of music or a musical lineage connected with the name of a particular person or place. Typically, what distinguishes one gharana from another is the unique style of presenting the music.

A certain style of music is called a gharana when three or more generations of musicians have preserved that style in public performances with a clear guru-shishya relationship being established. Needless to say, the method of teaching is traditional and carried forward for several years. A particular gharana also represents a certain ideology of music. This influences the manner in which the musician visualises a raga, or employs rhythmic elements, or presents a certain musical form.

For example, the Kirana gharana focuses on bringing out the emotional content through leisurely raga development and swara-prasthara, thus limiting their choice of ragas. The Agra gharana on the other hand has a wonderful repertoire of many varieties of musical compositions and rare ragas. The Jaipur gharana that concentrates on Khyal music, also uses rare ragas and is known for its intricate patterns in raga development. In the Benaras gharana, the Thumri form gets centerstage and the exponents of that gharana give emphasis on the lyrics and sing it in an emotionally evocative manner in order to bring out the meaning and the mood. The manner of singing Thumri by the Patiala gharana is markedly different, for they incorporate elements from the tappa form; this makes it different from the Khyal-rich Thumris of the Benaras gharana and the dance-oriented Thumris of the Lucknow gharana.

Gharanas are not restricted to singing alone. Even the various instruments have gharanas. For example, there are different tabla gharanas—Ajrada, Benaras, Delhi, Farukkabad, Lucknow, Punjab, etc. Similarly, there are gharanas for pakhawaj, sitar, sarod, etc.

Exponents of different gharanas have their own unique styles of singing the Khyal. There are variations in how much they emphasise and how they enunciate the lyrics of the bandish, when they sing sthayi and antara, whether to sing Alap in the beginning or not, what sort of improvisation to employ, how much of the rhythmic component to bring in, and so forth.

In the following pages, we list out alphabetically the gharanas and some of the major exponents, along with relevant information and photographs.

AGRA GHARANA

Agra gharana is noted as the second wonder of Agra, only after the elegant Taj Mahal. The founders of this gharana owe much to the dhrupad-dhammar singers, as it was from them that the Agra gharana members bestowed the major portion of their skillfulness. However, borrowing ingenuity from the dhrupadi singers, the Agra gharana was hugely successful in establishing a permanent position in musical history. Agra is the only gharana which boldly displays its dhrupadic roots. Agra gharana is said to have come from the Nauhar Bani, which is more than seven hundred years old. Nayak Gopal is said to be the founder of this gharana. The gharana was initially in the dhrupad-dhamar style but Ghagghe Khudabuksh (1790–1880) is said to have introduced the Khyal style of the Gwalior gharana into the Agra gharana. This is the only gharana that continues to sing dhrupad-dhamar along with nom-tom Alap, Khyal, Thumri, tappa, Tarana, and Hori, among others. According to Vilayat Hussain Khan, Agra gharana had two branches. One sprang from Shyamrang and Sarasrang around 1780, and the other from Imdad Khan around 1800. The former line was the one which produced a constant string of masters for over a hundred years, while the latter drifted towards light classical music like Thumri and Dadra.

Agra gharana is one of the most popular and highly reputed among the various contemporary gharanas. It absorbed attractive features from other gharanas and yet maintained its own inherent characteristics. It must be noted here that this particular gharana pertains to vocal music only, and has no counterpart in instrumental music; it has had a specific style in Dhrupad, Dhamar and Khyal.

Gayaki: The Agra gharana places great importance on developing forcefulness and deepness in the voice so that the notes are powerful and resonant. It places an emphasis on bold, full-throated and robust voice production. The gharana adopts the kind of voice production which relies on a flatter version of the vowel sound 'a', which makes its music agreeable to rhythmic variations and is best suited for a deep masculine voice.

Alap: Singers following Faiyaz Khan's style resort to the dhrupadic nom-tom Alap: long nom-tom Alap before commencing upon the Khyal composition, as practiced by Dhrupadiya.

Gamak: In tune with its dhrupadic origins, these singers use broad and powerful ornamentations (gamaks), extensive glides (meends), and resonant articulations of notes.

Khyal gayaki: This is a dhrupad-based development of Khyal. There is a greater emphasis on the purity of the raga and very little use of 'lighter' improvisational tools like Khatka and Murki.

Emphasis on the Bandish: Similar to the Gwalior gharana, the Agra singers also emphasise the importance of the bandish and its methodical exposition. The Bandish is well-enunciated with a clear and lyrical rendition of the text of the song.

Badhat: Importance is given to bol-Alap. Development of the raga is on the basis of the raga-phrases and rhythm for 'Swara-Badhat'. It employs Thumri-like Bol-Banav phrases in Chhota Khyal instead of long Alap laya-based ones.

The singers of this gharana are also great masters of the laya-kari or rhythmic content. In fact, laya-kari is the lasting foundation on which the singers build the structure of the bandish. When performed by the best musicians, the dialogue between the singer and the tabla player often turns into a dramatic event. Their tihayis are eagerly awaited, as are their stylish ways of arriving at the same (first beat), by building the listener's anticipation.

Founders: Nayak Gopal, Haji Sujan Khan, Ghagghe Khuda Baksh

Exponents: Faiyaz Khan, Vilayat Hussain Khan, Latafat Hussein Khan, Dinkar Kakini, Jitendra Abhisheki

BENARAS GHARANA

The Benaras gharana evolved because of the great lilting style of khyal singing known by Thumri singers of Benaras and Gaya. The song's lyrics are ornamented in order to emphasise their meaning. The Thumris of the Benaras gharana are Khyal-dominated. The Benaras gharana is more than seven hundred years old but it was revived in the past century by Siddheshwari Devi.

Founder: Gopal Mishra

Exponents: Rasoolan Bai, Badi Moti Bai, Siddheswari Devi, Mahadev Mishra, Girija Devi, Rajan and Sajan Mishra

BHENDIBAZAAR GHARANA

Dilawar Hussain Khan created the Bhendibazaar gharana. His three sons, Chhajjoo Khan, Nazeer Khan and Khadim Hussain Khan (the founders of Bhendibazaar gharana) shifted in the year 1870 from Bijnaur, near Moradabad in Uttar Pradesh, to Mumbai. It was called 'Behind the Bazaar' by the British, which transformed into Bhendibazaar. Chajjoo Khan, Nazeer Khan, and Khadim Hussain Khan received musical training initially from their father and later from Inayat Hussain Khan (Rampur-Sahaswan gharana) and Inayat Khan (Dagar gharana). The three brothers developed their own unique style and became famous as musicians from Bhendibazaar; their style was called 'Bhendibazaar gayaki'. However, this school did not just find things smoothly; they had to toil for it. And the man behind it all is Aman Ali Khan. Otherwise, a man of humble and reticent disposition, Aman Ali had a mellifluous voice and was a gifted composer. He wrote many songs that are sung even to this day. He adopted Khyal singing and popularised the emphasis on rhythm during the swaraprasthara. He was deeply influenced by many aspects of South Indian classical music, particularly the singing of complex solfa structures in a musically powerful manner. Along with Abdul Karim Khan of the Kirana gharana,

Aman Ali popularised sargam singing during the elaboration of a melodic idea.

Specifications of Bhendibazaar gharana: The gharana emphasises the use of delicate aesthetic tonal inflexions involving quick slides from one note to another, and also the use of Merukh and method of singing notes and note combinations. Complex merukh and combinations are incorporated in the elaboration of the raga as well as ornamentations borrowed from Carnatic music. The swaraprasthara is sung with a great emphasis on the aesthetic quality of music. According to M.R. Gautam, this gharana used sargam for the first time in Hindustani music in large measure and popularised it. Today this has become an almost necessary feature of Hindustani Classical music. Emphasis is placed on the correct enunciation and articulation of the lyric of the composition. Another special feature is the beauty of the swara-structure of the Khyals with special emphasis on their literary aspect. The words of the Khyal are beautifully woven into the raga and the tala, creating a mesmerising atmosphere. This gharana emphasises on breath control and the singing of long passages in a single breath.

Rich poetic bandishes: Most of the compositions of this gharana are gems of poetry and fine pieces of literature. The most significant characteristic of this gharana is that it specialises in Madhya Laya Khyal. The exponents of this gharana seldom sing vilambit Khyals. With the madhyalaya khyal they do all their raga, tala and tana development.

Founder: Chhajju Khan, Nazir Khan, Khadim Hussain Khan.

Exponents: Aman Ali Khan, Shashikala Koratkar, Anjanibai Malpekar, Trimbakrao D. Janorikar, Ramesh Laxman Nadkarni, Shivkumar Shukla, Master Navran Nagpurkar, Suhasini Koratkar.

DELHI GHARANA

Tanras Khan and Shabbu Khan are the primary representatives of the Delhi gharana, which is marked by a mellifluous rendition of ragas in an expansive manner, and richly ornate bandishes.

Founder: Mamman Khan

Exponents: Chand Khan, Usman Khan, Hilal Ahmed Khan, Nasir Ahmed Khan, Iqbal Ahmed Khan, Krishna Bisht

MEWATI GHARANA

The famous Mewati gharana came into existence during the later part of the nineteenth century, in Jodhpur. It was started by Ghagge Nazir Khan. Consequently, it is also known sometimes as the Jodhpur gharana or the Jaipur-Mewati gharana. Ghagge Nazir Khan was born in Mewat. Since his time, six generations of musicians have contributed towards the progress of the Mewati gharana. This name comes from the region where it originated – the Mewar region of Rajasthan. This gharana has a blend of both Hindu and Muslim influences. There is a strong focus on the mood of the melodic idea and it is hailed as bhava-pradhaana sangeeta. It is rich in ornamentation and lays emphasis on bhakti. With a history of more than 150 years, the Mewati gharana continues to be one of the most popular in Hindustani music.

Ghagge Nazir Khan is said to have passed on his legacy to Nathulal and Chimanlal. Nathulal taught his nephew, Motiram, who was the father of Pandit Jasraj - one of the most prominent torchbearers of the Mewati tradition in the last five to six decades. Jasraj's singing style is ornate and lyrically rich. He places great emphasis on the lyrics of the composition; their meaning, poetic content, and mood are brought out powerfully within the framework of the raga. He was responsible for bringing Haveli Sangeet and music from the Vaishnava temples in North India into his concerts, thus popularising them. The unique bhava-praadhaanya of the Mewati gharana gives it a unique place.

Special features of gayaki: The roots of the gayaki are in the Gwalior and Delhi gharanas, but the Mewati gharana has its own uniqueness.

Voice quality: Bold and clear voice capable of singing freely in all the three octaves. Importance is given to nom-tam Alap and to both sargam and aakaar. There is extensive use of ornamental techniques like Meend, Ghaseet, Ghamak. The ornamentations used in this gharana are known for their smoothness.

Bandish: Emphasis is placed on the lyrics of the bandish; through its words, emotional music was written. Importance is also given to mood (Rasa, Bhaava).

Important ragas: Jaiwanti Todi, Din ki Puriya, Odhav Bageshree, Khamaj Bahaar and Bhavani Bahar.

Founders: Ghagge Nazir Khan, Wahid Khan

Exponents: Motiram, Maniram, Pandit Jasraj, Sanjeev Abhyankar

PATIALA GHARANA

Primarily a sarangi gharana, the Patiala gharana gained fame as a vocal gharana due to the efforts of the renowned singer Bade Ghulam Ali Khan.

Patiala gharana is well-known for its lively and instantly entertaining gayaki. This is a style which incorporates almost every known tool of embellishment in Khyal, making it immediately appealing to all types of listeners. The singers of this gharana pioneered the powerful and intricate style of singing within the strict framework of Khyal. This gharana was founded by Ali Baksh and Fateh Ali, who were brothers and were famously known as 'Aliya-Fattu.' They had their musical training in Khyal and dhrupad under Miyan Kallu, a famous sarangi player in the court of Patiala. Aliya-Fattu were also known as Colonel (Karnail) and General (Jarnail) due to their forceful way of singing superfast taans.

The greatest star in the sky of the Patiala gharana is undoubtedly Bade Ghulam Ali Khan. After initial training from his father, he learnt from Miyan Kallu and further developed on his own. Apart from popularising the Patiala gharana, he also created the Punjab ang of Thumri singing. He was a powerful singer not just in the strongly classical Khyal form but also in light-classical forms like Thumri.

This gharana is famous for the singing of taans, which are intricate, rhythmic, and complicated. The emphasis is on singing from the nabhi and not from the throat. The audava-audava ragas are prominent in this gharana. The stress on the embellishments of the raga makes it innovative and unique.

Specifications of gayaki: Mellifluous and resonant voice production. The voice culture of Patiala gharana employs the use of a strong and full-throated voice. Its specialty lies in the use of rich, sweet, melodious and intricate use of notes in three octaves. The use of notes in analytical style is expressive. There are the minimal differences which distinguish this style from other gharanas.

Compositions being the basis of a gharana, Patiala is known for short and artistic khyal compositions that showcase the nature of its gayaki. The crisp, short, and impressive compositions are enriched with khatka, murki, kana, swar, drut laya and very intricate tans. The use of firat and sapaat tans enhances the beauty of this style. The Patiala gharana compositions are unique and have a distinctive flavour. This style emphasises fluent singing with a focus on the right articulation of swaras and an understanding of the aesthetics. It uses a lot of intricate tappa singing in the rendition of faster phrases and in the swaraprastharas.

The gayaki of the Patiala gharana—which has its roots in Punjab—has been influenced by Punjabi folk music. The use of these elements makes this style distinct from other gharanas. In this style, equal importance is given to melody and rhythm. The singers of this gharana are skilled in rendering light-classical musical forms like Bhajan, Thumri, and Dadra.

It is typical for musicians to use Behlava and Sargam during the transition from the Badhat stage to the Tana stage. The tans sung by the exponents of the Patiala gharana are exciting, especially given the speed and energy with which they are sung. This form has been labelled a taan-baazi style due to its inordinate fondness for fast phrases and rich ornamentation.

It employs Alankarik, Vakra (zigzag) and Phirat Tana in abundance. It also uses occasional Shadja Parivartan, or tonic transposition techniques during Sargam Tana.

Founders: Fateh Ali Khan, Ali Baksh

Exponents: Bade Ghulam Ali Khan, Barkat Ali Khan, Amanat Ali Khan, Munnawar Ali Khan, Prashun Banerjee, Meera Chatterjee, Jagadish Prasad, Begum Akhtar, Parveen Sultana, Ajoy Chakrabarty, Raza Ali Khan, Shiv Dayal Batish, Vasantrao Deshpande, Nirmala Aroon, Farida Khanum, Ghulam Ali

RAMPUR-SAHASWAN GHARANA

Rampur-Sahaswan gharana was established by Mehboob Khan's son, Inayat Hussain Khan, who was the son-in-law of Haddu Khan (of Gwalior fame). Mehboob Khan was a Khyal singer and vainika in the court of Rampur. Inayat Hussain Khan was a disciple of Bahadur Hussain Khan; he also learnt from his father-in-law, Haddu Khan. The Rampur-Sahaswan gharana is considered an offshoot of the Gwalior gharana. Some of the later maestros also imbibed some elements of the Agra gharana into this. Inayat Khan's siblings were beenkars in the court of the Rampur nawab. Though he was trained in Gwalior gayaki, Inayat Khan learnt dhrupad and settled in the court of Rampur. Since he hailed from the village of Sahaswan, the gharana came to be called Rampur-Sahaswan. In the previous century, it was Mustaq Hussain Khan who took forward the style with his widespread knowledge of music. Apart from learning from Haider Khan and Inayat Khan, he was also trained in Dhrupad-

Dhamar by Wazir Khan. He had wide sweep and ranges with a great command over all technical aspects of Khyal. Another reputed singer of this gharana was Nissar Hussain Khan, who was renowned for this rendition of the Tarana form.

Specifications of gayaki: Rampur Sahaswan is an offshoot of the Gwalior gharana, and shares its major characteristics. This gharana requires a full-throated and clear voice that freely move in three octaves. It employs methodical and structured rendition of the sthayi and the antara, in keeping with the Gwalior heritage. Bandish is rendered carefully with special attention given to the lyrics. There is more emphasis on vilambit and madhyalaya Alaps. Taans and Taranas are unique in this gharana. In this style of singing, there is great emphasis on rhythmic patterns, clarity of swara, and stepwise development of raga elaboration.

The use of the lyrics of the song in all stages of the vilambit khyal is preferred to aakar. The words of the song, moreover, are presented in the natural order and overemphasis on any single word is generally avoided.

This gharana uses Bol-Alaps a lot. Bol-Alap refers to the elaboration of a raga using particular lines from the lyrics of the bandish in order to evoke a certain rasa (aesthetic experience) that is associated with that given raga. The musicians sing taans with great skill, clarity, force, and speed. The singers of this gharana are also masters of singing the Tarana musical form.

Founder: Inayat Khan

Exponents: Nissar Hussain Khan, Haider Khan, Mushtaq Hussain Khan, Kailas Chandra Dey Brihaspati, Sulochana Brihaspati, Ghulam Mustafa Khan, Hafeez Ahmed Khan, Rashid Khan, Naina Devi (also belongs to the Benaras gharana)

GWALIOR GHARANA

Being the oldest, most expansive, and long-lasting of the extant gharanas, Gwalior gharana is widely recognised as being the parent of the other gharanas. In the reigning period of Raja Man Singh Tomar (fifteenth century), Gwalior was the seat of Dhrupad. It then became the parent gharana for Khyal in the eighteenth century. It is also believed that Nathhan Pir Baksh, who was supported by the king of the Gwalior State, Naresh Jayaji Rao, created this gharana. According to late Vilayat Husaain Khan, this gharana originated from Abdullah Khan and Kadir Bux Khan, who were brothers. They were deemed singers of Khyals and were considered Ustads. They were said to hail from a village near Delhi, but their ancestors came from Gwalior and had very close connections with the Gwalior court. These two brothers were court musicians in the time of Maharaja Jhinkuji Rao Scindia. After them came the two sons of Kadir Bux-Nathan Khan and Pir Bux. They were then taught by their father and eventually turned into experts at rendering Khyals. The special feature of their gayaki was the gravity and depth of their exposition. They were also known for their unprecedented command over tala. They lived in the time of the Maharaja Daulatrao Scindia. The two brothers then permanently settled in Gwalior and started the parampara of training their children.

Singers of this gharana prefer well-known ragas over rare ones and are renowned for their simplicity. The elaboration of the raga is limited and embellishments are added to enhance the beauty of the raga; vilambit laya is avoided. Emphasis is placed on the meaning of the lyric. The exponents of the Gwalior gharana believe that the melodic beauty of the raga is given by the bandish and therefore they present the musical composition at the core of their exposition. They sing the asthayi segment twice before going to the antara, which is then followed by swaravistara in madhya-laya. This medium tempo rendition of the notes spans between the madhyama of the mandra-sthayi to the panchama of the tara-sthayi, following the structure of the aroha and avaroha of the raga. The behlava is divided into two sections, the asthayi (from the mandra madhyama to shadja) and the antara (from the madhya-sthayi madhyama or panchama to the tara Panchama). This is followed by what is known as the Dugun ka Alap, in which groups of two or four swara combinations are rendered in quick succession while maintaining the same basic laya. Then comes the Bol Alap, in which the musician sings the different words of the lyric in different ways; this is followed by Murkis, in which the singer sings the swaras with gamakas in a faster tempo. Then comes the Bol taan, in which melodic sequences are formed with the lyrics of the bandish. In this gharana, the Sapat taan has an important place; it refers to rendering the swaras in a straight sequence and in the vilambit laya. Under the purview of the Gwalior school, both dhrupad and Khyal singing developed and therefore we find a lot of overlap.

Founders: Hassu Khan, Haddu Khan, Nathu Khan

Exponents: Rehmat Khan, Balkrishnabua Ichalkaranjikar, Vishnu Digambar Paluskar, Omkarnath Thakur, Vinayak Rao Patwardhan, Narayanrao Vyas, Ramkrishnabua Vaze, Krishna Rao Shankar Pandit, D V Paluskar, B R Deodhar, Kumar Gandharva, N Rajam, D K Datar, Sharad Sate, Vidyadhar Vyas, Veena Sahasrabuddhe, Ulhas Kashalkar, Malini Rajurkar, Gururao Deshpande, Meeta Pandit

INDORE GHARANA

The Indore gharana is one of the prominent vocal gharanas of Hindustani music and was created by the renowned singer Amir Khan. The great maestro studied the singing styles of renowned masters such as Abdul Wahid Khan, Aman Ali Khan, Rajab Ali Khan, and Abdul Karim Khan for several years and finally amalgamated the essence of their styles with his own creativity and intellectual approach; from that, he created the famous Indore gharana. The characteristics of the Indore gharana are vilambit laya Alaps and slow development of raga, emphasis on the lower register, lenience towards the expansive and somber ragas, the use of meaningful pauses between the notes, and clear pronunciation of the lyric. It is mostly introspective in nature.

Founder: Amir Khan

Exponents: Amarnath, Shankar Lal Mishra, Ram Narain, Sultan Khan, Kankana Banerjee, Srikant Bakre, Singh Bandhu, Purvi Mukherjee, Gokulotsav Maharaj

JAIPUR-ATRAULI GHARANA

The Jaipur-Atrauli gharana, which is also known as the Jaipur gharana, is a popular Khyal gharana that was founded by the great maestro Alladiya Khan (1855–1946) in the later part of the nineteenth century. It evolved from dhrupad as well as from haveli sangeet. This gharana is known for its wide-ranging repertoire of ragas as well as its remarkable layakari. A lot of ornamentation is included in the taans, making it rich and intricate. Perhaps no other style of singing placed as much emphasis on the aesthetics and laykari while singing the bol-Alaps and bol-taans as the Jaipur-Atrauli gharana.

Alladiya Khan's family belonged to Atrauli near Aligarh, and later migrated to Jaipur, giving the gharana its name. This gharana is more than a hundred and fifty years old. It has had assorted musicians of eminence. Some of them became famous all over India, while others were greatly respected as knowledgeable musicians with pervasive repertoires. Among the various gharanas, the Jaipur-Atrauli has a special place as a highly intellectual and structured school of singing. It has captured generations of listeners with its unique style of presenting ragas by including complex melodic lines with intricate rhythmic patterns.

The gharana greatly evolved in the able hands of Alladiya Khan, a prominent exponent of this school of singing. Powerful laya patterns, elaboration of raga with complex ornamentation and movements, and traversing all three sthayis are typical of this school. It was in the later part of the nineteenth century that the Jaipur-Atrauli tradition emerged as a strong Khyal gharana, primarily due to the tireless efforts of Alladiya Khan. His ancestors, mostly singers, came from the village of Atrauli, near the town of Aligarh. They migrated to a small village near Jaipur and became a part of the royal court.

Ragas: The exponents of this school prefer intricate, rare, and complex ragas to the popular and less complex ones. There is a penchant for rare (mostly Salag and Sankirna) Ragas, i.e., Ragas neither commonly presented by the other gharana nor well-known to the concert-going public at large. Primary emphasis is on aesthetics relating to the form of the genre of the song, i.e., the artistic and intellectual variety of development of its various components such as Vistar, Bolbant, Layakari, Tanas.

Voice Quality: Full-throated voice production and use of chest voice.

Alap: Typical of this school is the elongated employment of open-throated akara singing in all three sthayis.

Development of the raga: Predominance of akara in the development of the raga, steady development of the melodic and rhythmic elements in an integrated manner, complicated swara patterns sung with accuracy and spontainety in madhya-laya, and unique approach to even familiar ragas are all the features of this cerebral and musically ornate gharana. Prominence of Tana and rhythmic Behlava in the course of Vistar.

Bandish: These are given less importance. Generally, they are short compositions. To a number of exponents of this gharana, the lyrics of the bandish are not very important and they focus more on the swara patterns and combinations rather than the literary aspect of the lyrics.

Structure of the Taans: This school has complicated taans with intricate gamakas. Against the backdrop of the rhythmic structure, the swaras move about in a tantalising and ornate manner. It employs short Penchdar (rolling or twisted/difficult) Tana even in Vistar portions. Alankaric and ornamental patterned Tanas. Unlike other gharanas, the singers of the Jaipur-Atrauli gharana rarely sing sargams or sargam taans while they elaborate on a raga.

Founders: Alladiya Khan

Exponents: Kesarbai Kerkar, Mogubai Kurdikar, Mallikarjun Mansur, Vamanrao Deshpande, Gajananrao Joshi, Nivruttibua Sarnaik, Kishori Amonkar, Padma Talwalkar, Shruti Sadolikar, Ashwini Bhide Deshpande

KIRANA GHARANA

The Kirana gharana gets its name from Abdul Karim Khan's birthplace, the town of Kirana near Kurukshetra. This gharana claims its origin from the famous Beenkar Bande Ali Khan. Late Abdul Karim Khan Sahib and Abdul Wahid Khan Saheb took this gharana to new heights with their caliber. The maestros who established this school of thought were primarily Sarangi players, and that had a huge influence on the performance of those exponents. It was Abdul Karim Khan who played a major role in the evolution of the Kirana gharana and gave it the exalted place it holds today.

The great maestro Abdul Waheed Khan reintroduced the vilambit laya in Khyal, something that attracted the common people towards the Khyal form. He brought in the rich combination of swaras for raga exposition. The Kirana gharana is an eclectic mix of tradition and modernity, fused in a bold and careful manner in order to appeal to audiences of various time periods. It has a lot of influence from the South Indian classical style of music.

Abdul Karim Khan introduced the sargam taan from Carnatic music and that gained a lot of popularity. The Kirana gharana flourished all through the twentieth century. Melodic voice production, sweetness of tone, and softer gamakas are typical of this school of music.

The Kirana gharana has several great exponents who attained widespread fame—Sawai Gandharva, Ramachandra Behrebua, Balakrishnabua Kapileshwari, Roshanara Begum, Heerabai Barodekar, Bhimsen Joshi, Gangubai Hangal, and many others. The Kirana gayaki brings out the emotion of the ragas in an evocative manner. Due to its emphasis on tone and emotion, it became hugely popular with all classes of society. The singers of this gharana use limited ragas and, as pointed out by the Marathi polymath Pu La Deshpande, they have a strong preference for ragas with a komal rishab (minor second).

Voice Quality: Voice production in this gharana is very distinct. Of the two registers in human voice—lower and upper—the upper is tirelessly developed, almost to the neglect of the lower. Vamanrao Deshpande, in his book *Indian Music Traditions - An Aesthetic Study of the Gharanas in Hindustani Music*, has in one place described the Kirana voice as 'delicate and tender; it resembles a soft silken thread and possesses a sharp point.'

Swara: The Kirana gharana emphasises the individual swaras. The Alap is developed in all three registers, but emphasis is on the higher octaves. To sing the swara as accurately as possible is what this gharana specialises in. Their entire attention is concentrated on singing in sur, and all their practical exercises are directed towards achieving this. The focus of the singers in this gharana is on swara development without much regard for tala.

Bandish: Complete statement of the Sthayi and Antara of both Vilambit as well as Drut Khyal is not done by some of the renowned musicians of this gharana, from which one has inevitably to ascertain that not much value is given by them to the composition they are singing. Famous singers of this gharana treat the sthayi and antara of a bandish in a fleeting manner and the composition is not given as much prominence as in the Gwalior or Agra gharanas.

Badhat: Badhat, or slow systematic development note by note, is another characteristic of this gharana. The students of Kirana gharana are taught swara exercises involving complicated arithmetical alterations and combinations. By practicing these exercises, they attain a commendable command over the swaras.

Alap: Alap-Pradhhan Gayaki, i.e., the style of singing heavily, relies on Alap. They also use a lot of Bol-Alaps, where a line or phrase from the lyrics of the bandish is used for developing melodic ideas (in the place of akaras). This gharana specialises in vilambit Alaps.

Founders: Abdul Karim Khan, Abdul Wahid Khan

Exponents: Sawai Gandharva, Sureshbabu Mane, Hirabhai Barodekar, Saraswati Rane, Gangubai Hangal, Begum Akhtar, Roshan Ara Begum, Basavaraj Rajguru, Firoz Dastur, Bhimsen Joshi, Fayyaz Ahmed Khan, Niaz Ahmed Khan, Manik Varma, Prabha Atre, Mashkoor Ali Khan

5

Rhythmic Concepts

The rhythmic concepts in Carnatic music are arguably the most developed and sophisticated in any musical tradition. The tala system which deals with the rhythmic cycles is very methodical and extremely well organised. Because of the musical freedom given to the performer in the Carnatic system, he can take a simple rhythmic cycle and further divide each beat into a number of subdivisions (pulses) and make it as complicated as he wants. There are other systems where the musician can create layers of rhythmic patterns in which each layer on its own is a different pattern, but the whole, when heard together, sounds complex. However, in Carnatic music, in a percussion ensemble (during the solo section), each performer creates his own complex rhythmic patterns depending on his virtuosic and creative capacity. Yet, despite each individual's ideas, he still stays within the same structure and framework set by the leader of the group (usually the mridangam player, when the typical ensemble consists of a mridangam, khanjira, ghatam and moorsing). Towards the end, when the entire ensemble plays together, they try to play similar patterns set by the leader to reach the end of the section in an exciting finale. This whole percussion solo section is known as tani avartanam. Similarly, some of the great tavil players, in their solo sections, also create some of the most difficult rhythmic patterns within their own traditional framework.

It is interesting to note that there are differences in the vocabulary of rhythmic patterns of the tavil and the mridangam player. Normally, the tavil is the traditional accompaniment for the nadaswaram, whereas the mridangam, khanjira and ghatam are the traditional accompaniments for vocal music and instruments like the veena, gotuvadyam, flute and violin.

The tala system is a system of rhythmic cycles. Each composition is based on a tala. This corresponds to the time signature in the Western classical system. In any Western notation, which is written in five lines called the staff, you will find the time signature denoted by two numbers, one above the other, placed next to the clef sign in the beginning of the staff. In the Carnatic system, before the composition, the name of the raga and the tala are mentioned, and the musician is expected to know the structure and division of the tala just by the name. The famous Sanskrit saying, *'Shruthi Mata Laya Pita'*—Shruthi (pitch) is the mother and Laya (rhythm) is the father—shows the importance of pitch and rhythm. These are the two main factors essential to Indian music.

In the olden days, talas were classified into marga (classical) and desi (folk, popular) talas. The five marga talas and hundred and twenty desi talas are mentioned in Sarangadeva's *Sangeeta Ratnakara* (early thirteenth century). It is believed that the marga talas existed from a much earlier time. Most of the desi talas figure in the system of hundred and eight classical talas which followed (this system came into existence in the post-Bharata period). These are now almost obsolete and used mainly for demonstration purposes. The longest of the hundred and eight talas, Simhanandana, has one hundred and twenty-eight beats per rhythmic cycle. Great musicians like Maha Vaidyanatha Iyer and Patnam Subramania Iyer have composed and performed compositions in this tala. This system of hundred and eight talas was based on six angas or components (anga means limbs), which are as follows:

TABLE 5.1

Attga (Component)	*No. of beats*	*Symbol*
1. Anudrutam	One beat or akshara	◡
2. Drutam	Two beats	0
3. Laghu	Four beats	|
4. Guru	Eight beats (equivalent to two laghus)	8
5. Plutam	Twelve beats (equivalent to three laghus)	$\overset{\mid}{8}$
6. Kakapadam	Sixteen beats (equivalent to four laghus)	+

This old system gave way to a simpler system of seven talas expanded to thirty-five talas. Purandara Dasa composed alankaras and gitams in these talas (see under Musical Forms).

Later, the great musical trinity of Tyagaraja, Muthuswami Dikshitar and Shyama Shastri also composed most of their compositions based on this system of talas. This is the most prevalent system today in the Carnatic tradition, along with another smaller group of talas known as chapu talas.

THE THIRTY-FIVE TALA SYSTEM

This system is based on seven talas (sapta talas). They use only the first three of the six components referred to earlier. They are the anudrutam, the drutam and the laghu.

The anudrutam is a clap and is one kriya (kriya means a signal made by the hand). The drutam is a clap (known as ghata) and a wave of the hand (known as usi). Each is a kriya, thus the drutam consists of two kriyas. The laghu is a clap and finger counts. The total number of kriyas in a laghu is the total of the clap and the number of finger counts used.

Each anga begins with a clap or beat. The clap is the only sabda (Sanskrit for sound) kriya. In other words, it is the only part of the anga which has a sound or is audible. All the other parts (wave and finger counts) are nisabda ('no sound') kriyas, or kriyas which are silent. No anga has more than one sabda kriya.

The seven basic talas are:

TABLE 5.2

	Tala		*Formula*
1	Dhruva	|O||	(one laghu, one drutam, two laghus)
2	Matya	|O|	(one laghu, one drutam, one laghu)
3	Rupaka	O|	(one drutam, one laghu)
4	Jhampa	|◡O	(one laghu, one anudrutam, one drutam)
5	Triputa	|O O	(one laghu, two drutams)
6	Ata	||O O	(two laghus, two drutams)
7	Eka	|	(one laghu)

Thus a tala has three angas (elements):

a. Anudrutam: one beat (one clap)
b. Drutam: two beats (one clap and wave)
c. Laghu: three, four, five, seven, or nine beats (one clap and finger counts)

The drutam and the anudrutam are constant and the laghu is variable.

The laghu can be of five jatis (types):

TABLE 5.3

	Jati	*Number of Beats*	*Symbol*
1	Tisra	Three	$\|_3$
2	Chatusra	Four	$\|_4$
3	Khanda	Five	$\|_5$
4	Misra	Seven	$\|_7$
5	Sankirna	Nine	$\|_9$

Thus, by varying each laghu, each type of tala gives rise to five different varieties of the same tala. Let us take the simplest tala—Eka tala—to explain this. The tala consists of only one laghu. Hence, by varying the jati, we get five different variations of the tala.

TABLE 5.4

1	Tisra Jati Eka tala	three beats	(one clap + two finger counts)
2	Chatusra Jati Eka tala	four beats	(one clap + three finger counts)
3	Khanda Jati Eka tala	five beats	(one clap + four finger counts)
4	Misra Jati Eka tala	seven beats	(one clap + six finger counts)
5	Sankirna Jati Eka tala	nine beats	(one clap + eight finger counts)

Similarly, by varying the laghus in the other types of talas, we get five different varieties from each tala. Thus, we get 7 x 5 = 35 talas. The individual names of the thirty-five talas are not in common use. They are known in terms of the basic tala with their corresponding jatis, for example, Khanda Jati Triputa tala, Tisra Jati Dhruva tala and so on. It is important to note that, within each variety of tala, the laghu must necessarily be of the same jati throughout, that is, in Khanda Jati Dhruva tala, all three laghus must be of the khanda jati (I_5).

The chart below shows the thirty-five talas with their respective symbols and the division of the beats in each cycle of tala.

TABLE 5.5

	Tala	*Symbol*	*Division*	*Total Beats*
1	Tisra Jati Dhruva	$\vert_3 O \vert_3 \vert_3$	3+2+3+3	11
2	Chatusra Jati Dhruva	$\vert_4 O \vert_4 \vert_4$	4+2+4+4	14
3	Khanda Jati Dhruva	$\vert_5 O \vert_5 \vert_5$	5+2+5+5	17
4	Misra Jati Dhruva	$\vert_7 O \vert_7 \vert_7$	7+2+7+7	23
5	Sankirna Jati Dhruva	$\vert_9 O \vert_9 \vert_9$	9+2+9+9	29
6	Tisra Jati Matya	$\vert_3 O \vert_3$	3+2+3	8

	Tala	*Symbol*	*Division*	*Total Beats*
7	Chatusra Jati Matya	$|_4 O |_4$	4+2+4	10
8	Khanda Jati Matya	$|_5 O |_5$	5+2+5	12
9	Misra Jati Matya	$|_7 O |_7$	7+2+7	16
10	Sankirna Jati Matya	$|_9 O |_9$	9+2+9	20
11	Tisra Jati Rupaka	$O |_3$	2+3	5
12	Chatusra Jati Rupaka	$O |_4$	2+4	6
13	Khanda Jati Rupaka	$O |_5$	2+5	7
14	Misra Jati Rupaka	$O |_7$	2+7	9
15	Sankirna Jati Rupaka	$O |_9$	2+9	11
16	Tisra Jati Jhampa	$|_3 \smile O$	3+1+2	6
17	Chatusra Jati Jhampa	$|_4 \smile O$	4+1+2	7
18	Khanda Jati Jhampa	$|_5 \smile O$	5+1+2	8
19	Misra Jati Jhampa	$|_7 \smile O$	7+1+2	10
20	Sankirna Jati Jhampa	$|_9 \smile O$	9+1+2	12
21	Tisra Jati Triputa	$|_3 OO$	3+2+2	7
22	Chatusra Jati Triputa	$|_4 OO$	4+2+2	8
23	Khanda Jati Triputa	$|_5 OO$	5+2+2	9
24	Misra Jati Triputa	$|_7 OO$	7+2+2	11
25	Sankirna Jati Triputa	$|_9 OO$	9+2+2	13
26	Tisra Jati Ata	$|_3 |_3 OO$	3+3+2+2	10
27	Chatusra Jati Ata	$|_4 |_4 OO$	4+4+2+2	12
28	Khanda Jati Ata	$|_5 |_5 OO$	5+5+2+2	14
29	Misra Jati Ata	$|_7 |_7 OO$	7+7+2+2	18
30	Sankirna Jati Ata	$|_9 |_9 OO$	9+9+2+2	22
31	Tisra Jati Eka	$|_3$	3	3
32	Chatusra Jati Eka	$|_4$	4	4
33	Khanda Jati Eka	$|_5$	5	5
34	Misra Jati Eka	$|_7$	7	7
35	Sankirna Jati Eka	$|_9$	9	9

Several talas have the same number of beats, for example, Tisra Jati Matya, Khanda Jati Jhampa and Chatusra Jati Triputa all consist of an eight-beat cycle, but they differ from one another in the treatment because the components and/or their arrangements differ and hence the emphasis is placed on different points in the cycle, depending on the angas.

Just as varying the laghus gives rise to thirty-five talas from the basic seven talas, we can further expand each tala into five different varieties by varying the gati. Gati or nadai stands for the number of pulses that each beat is divided into. Like the laghu, these are also of five types: tisra (three), chatusra (four), khanda (five), misra (seven) and sankirna (nine). Thus, by varying the number of pulses per beat, each tala gives rise to another five varieties, giving us a total of 35 × 5 = 175 talas.

The following chart shows how the thirty-five different talas are expanded into 175 varieties by changing the number of pulses per beat (gati or nadai).

TABLE 5.6

Tala	*Total Beats*	*Nadai*	*Total No. of Pulses*
Tisra Jati Dhruva	3+2+3+3=11	Tisra	11 x 3 = 33
”	”	Chatusra	11 x 4 = 44
”	”	Khanda	11x 5 = 55
”	”	Misra	11 x 7 = 77
”	”	Sankirna	11 x 9 = 99
Chatusra Jati Dhruva	4+2+4+4=14	Tisra	14 x 3 = 42
”	”	Chatusra	14 x 4 = 56
”	”	Khanda	14 x 5 = 70
”	”	Misra	14 x 7 = 98
”	”	Sankirna	14 x 9 = 126

Tala	*Total Beats*	*Nadai*	*Total No. of Pulses*
Khanda Jati Dhruva	5+2+5+5=17	Tisra	17 x 3 = 51
"	"	Chatusra	17 x 4 = 68
"	"	Khanda	17 x 5 = 85
"	"	Misra	17 x 7 = 119
"	"	Sankirna	17 x 9 = 153
Misra Jati Dhruva	7+2+7+7=23	Tisra	23 x 3 = 69
"	"	Chatusra	23 x 4 = 92
"	"	Khanda	23 x 5 = 115
"	"	Misra	23 x 7 = 161
"	"	Sankirna	23 x 9 = 207
Sankirna Jati Dhruva	9+2+9+9=29	Tisra	29 x 3 = 87
"	"	Chatusra	29 x 4 = 116
"	"	Khanda	29 x 5 = 145
"	"	Misra	29 x 7 = 203
"	"	Sankirna	29 x 9 = 261
Tisra Jati Matya	3+2+3=8	Tisra	8 x 3 = 24
"	"	Chatusra	8 x 4 = 32
"	"	Khanda	8 x 5 = 40
"	"	Misra	8 x 7 = 56
"	"	Sankirna	8 x 9 = 72
Chatusra Jati Matya	4+2+4= 10	Tisra	10 x 3 = 30
"	"	Chatusra	10 x 4 = 40
"	"	Khanda	10 x 5 = 50
"	"	Misra	10 x 7 = 70
"	"	Sankima	10 x 9 = 90
Khanda Jati Matya	5+2+5=12	Tisra	12 x 3 = 36
"	"	Chatusra	12 x 4 = 48
"	"	Khanda	12 x 5 = 60
"	"	Misra	12 x 7 = 84
"	"	Sankirna	12 x 9 = 108

Tala	*Total Beats*	*Nadai*	*Total No. of Pulses*
Misra Jati Matya	7+2+7=16	Tisra	16 x 3 = 48
"	"	Chatusra	16 x 4 = 64
"	"	Khanda	16 x 5 = 80
"	"	Misra	16 x 7 = 112
"	"	Sankirna	16 x 9 = 144
Sankirna Jati Matya	9+2+9=20	Tisra	20 x 3 = 60
"	"	Chatusra	20 x 4 = 80
"	"	Khanda	20 x 5 = 100
"	"	Misra	20 x 7 = 140
"	"	Sankirna	20 x 9 = 180
Tisra Jati Rupaka	2+3=5	Tisra	5 x 3 = 15
"	"	Chatusra	5 x 4 = 20
"	"	Khanda	5 x 5 = 25
"	"	Misra	5 x 7 = 35
"	"	Sankirna	5 x 9 = 45
Chatusra Jati Rupaka	2+4=6	Tisra	6 x 3 = 18
"	"	Chatusra	6 x 4 = 24
"	"	Khanda	6 x 5 = 30
"	"	Misra	6 x 7 = 42
"	"	Sankirna	6 x 9 = 54
Khanda Jati Rupaka	2+5=7	Tisra	7 x 3 = 21
"	"	Chatusra	7 x 4 = 28
"	"	Khanda	7 x 5 = 35
"	"	Misra	7 x 7 = 49
"	"	Sankirna	7 x 9 = 63
Misra Jati Rupaka	2+7=9	Tisra	9 x 3 = 27
"	"	Chatusra	9 x 4 = 36
"	"	Khanda	9 x 5 = 45
"	"	Misra	9 x 7 = 63
"	"	Sankirna	9 x 9 = 81

Tala	*Total Beats*	*Nadai*	*Total No. of Pulses*
Sankirna Jati Rupaka	2+9=11	Tisra	11 x 3 = 33
"	"	Chatusra	11 x 4 = 44
"	"	Khanda	11 x 5 = 55
"	"	Misra	11 x 7 = 77
"	"	Sankirna	11 x 9 = 99
Tisra Jati Jhampa	3+1+2=6	Tisra	6 x 3 = 18
"	"	Chatusra	6 x 4 = 24
"	"	Khanda	6 x 5 = 30
"	"	Misra	6 x 7 = 42
"	"	Sankirna	6 x 9 = 54
Chatusra Jati Jhampa	4+1+2=7	Tisra	7 x 3 = 21
"	"	Chatusra	7 x 4 = 28
"	"	Khanda	7 x 5 = 35
"	"	Misra	7 x 7 = 49
"	"	Sankirna	7 x 9 = 63
Khanda Jati Jhampa	5+1+2=8	Tisra	8 x 3 = 24
"	"	Chatusra	8 x 4 = 32
"	"	Khanda	8 x 5 = 40
"	"	Misra	8 x 7 = 56
"	"	Sankirna	8 x 9 = 72
Misra Jati Jhampa	7+1+2=10	Tisra	10 x 3 = 30
"	"	Chatusra	10 x 4 = 40
"	"	Khanda	10 x 5 = 50
"	"	Misra	10 x 7 = 70
"	"	Sankirna	10 x 9 = 90
Sankirna Jati Jhampa	9+1+2=12	Tisra	12 x 3 = 36
"	"	Chatusra	12 x 4 = 48
"	"	Khanda	12 x 5 = 60
"	"	Misra	12 x 7 = 84
"	"	Sankirna	12 x 9 = 108

Tala	*Total Beats*	*Nadai*	*Total No. of Pulses*
Tisra Jati Triputa	3+2+2=7	Tisra	7 x 3 = 21
”	”	Chatusra	7 x 4 = 28
”	”	Khanda	7 x 5 = 35
”	”	Misra	7 x 7 = 49
”	”	Sankirna	7 x 9 = 63
Chatusra Jati Triputa	4+2+2=8	Tisra	8 x 3 = 24
”	”	Chatusra	8 x 4 = 32
”	”	Khanda	8 x 5 = 40
”	”	Misra	8 x 7 = 56
”	”	Sankirna	8 x 9 = 72
Khanda Jati Triputa	5+2+2=9	Tisra	9 x 3 = 27
”	”	Chatusra	9 x 4 = 36
”	”	Khanda	9 x 5 = 45
”	”	Misra	9 x 7 = 63
”	”	Sankirna	9 x 9 = 81
Misra Jati Triputa	7+2+2=11	Tisra	11 x 3 = 33
”	”	Chatusra	11 x 4 = 44
”	”	Khanda	11 x 5 = 55
”	”	Misra	11 x 7 = 77
”	”	Sankirna	11 x 9 = 99
Sankirna Jati Triputa	9+2+2=13	Tisra	13 x 3 = 39
”	”	Chatusra	13 x 4 = 52
”	”	Khanda	13 x 5 = 65
”	”	Misra	13 x 7 = 91
”	”	Sankirna	13 x 9 = 117
Tisra Jati Ata	3+3+2+2=10	Tisra	10 x 3 = 30
”	”	Chatusra	10 x 4 = 40
”	”	Khanda	10 x 5 = 50
”	”	Misra	10 x 7 = 70
”	”	Sankirna	10 x 9 = 90

Tala	*Total Beats*	*Nadai*	*Total No. of Pulses*
Chatusra Jati Ata	4+4+2+2=12	Tisra	12 x 3 = 36
"	"	Chatusra	12 x 4 = 48
"	"	Khanda	12 x 5 = 60
"	"	Misra	12 x 7 = 84
"	"	Sankirna	12 x 9 = 108
Khanda Jati Ata	5+5+2+2=14	Tisra	14 x 3 = 42
"	"	Chatusra	14 x 4 = 56
"	"	Khanda	14 x 5 = 70
"	"	Misra	14 x 7 = 98
"	"	Sankirna	14 x 9 = 126
Misra Jati Ata	7+7+2+2=18	Tisra	18 x 3 = 54
"	"	Chatusra	18 x 4 = 72
"	"	Khanda	18 x 5 = 90
"	"	Misra	18 x 7 = 126
"	"	Sankirna	18 x 9 = 162
Sankirna Jati Ata	9+9+2+2=22	Tisra	22 x 3 = 66
"	"	Chatusra	22 x 4 = 88
"	"	Khanda	22 x 5 = 110
"	"	Misra	22 x 7 = 154
"	"	Sankirna	22 x 9 = 198
Tisra Jati Eka	3	Tisra	3 x 3 = 9
"	"	Chalusra	3 x 4 = 12
"	"	Khanda	3 x 5 = 15
"	"	Misra	3 x 7 = 21
"	"	Sankirna	3 x 9 = 27
Chatusra Jati Eka	4	Tisra	4 x 3 = 12
"	"	Chatusra	4 x 4 = 16
"	"	Khanda	4 x 5 = 20
"	"	Misra	4 x 7 = 28
"	"	Sankirna	4 x 9 = 36

Tala	*Total Beats*	*Nadai*	*Total No. of Pulses*
Khanda Jati Eka	5	Tisra	5 x 3 = 15
"	"	Chatusra	5 x 4 = 20
"	"	Khanda	5 x 5 = 25
"	"	Misra	5 x 7 = 35
"	"	Sankirna	5 x 9 = 45
Misra Jati Eka	7	Tisra	7 x 3 = 21
"	"	Chatusra	7 x 4 = 28
"	"	Khanda	7 x 5 = 35
"	"	Misra	7 x 7 = 49
"	"	Sankirna	7 x 9 = 63
Sankirna Jati Eka	9	Tisra	9 x 3 = 27
"	"	Chatusra	9 x 4 = 36
"	"	Khanda	9 x 5 = 45
"	"	Misra	9 x 7 = 63
"	"	Sankirna	9 x 9 = 81

When you write the name of the tala, it is usually indicated by:

(1) the jati or type (which refers to laghu);
(2) the name of the basic tala;
(3) the gati or nadai (which indicates the subdivision into number of pulses per beat).

For example, Tisra Jati Eka tala, Khanda gati (or nadai) indicates Eka tala (with one laghu) consisting of three beats (Tisra jati), each beat subdivided into five pulses per beat (Khanda nadai), thus giving a total of fifteen pulses per cycle of the tala.

Thus, by varying each of the thirty-five talas in the same manner, we get 175 talas in all. One major difference in the jati and the gati is that jati refers only to the laghu and affects the total number of its beats, whereas the gati affects every beat of every anga of the tala, each beat divided into an equal number of pulses or subdivisions.

In a Carnatic music concert, if the main artist is a singer, he indicates the tala cycle by different hand gestures and movements. This acts as a reference point for the accompanists, the violinist and the mridangist, who use both hands to play their instruments, unlike the singer whose hands are free. Sometimes, it is not uncommon for the violinist or the percussionist to keep the cycle with his foot. For example, for the Adi tala; (eight-beat cycle) which is divided into 4+2+2 beats (I_4 0 0) he moves his feet for the first, fifth and seventh beats, indicating the beginning of the three components of this particular tala. During a concert performance in India, the audience participates by keeping the tala cycle with hand gestures. Often, the main artist can depend on a musically knowledgeable listener indicating the tala cycle and, sometimes, instrumental soloists bring their own tala-keeper. In a Western symphonic or chamber orchestral concert, the conductor stands in front of the orchestra, guiding it with different gestures. His role is the most important in an orchestra and he is expected to know the structure of the composition with its nuances and phrasing, the different entries and exits of the various instruments and the dynamics and tempi of different sections in detail. He is also expected to create a balance between different instrumental sections so that the audience can hear the melodic structure or the horizontal movement in balance with the vertical movement, which is mostly the harmonic structure. This is why the same orchestral composition performed by the same orchestra sounds different under different conductors, in relation to their understanding and interpretation of the composition and their own individual inputs.

In the Indian system, the role of the tala-keeper (if other than the main vocalist) is mainly to show the different angas and tempo of the rhythmic cycle within the guidelines set by the main artist.

During the early stages of learning, even an instrumentalist is taught to sing the compositions, keeping the tala while singing, or, in the case of a percussionist, reciting the different percussion compositions keeping the tala. This helps in developing a steady sense of rhythm and a feel for the structure and phrasing of the composition within the strict framework of the tala cycle. As a result, when instrumentalists play these compositions later, they can understand and interpret them better, emphasising different sections according to the structure of the composition, even without keeping the tala. The term used for the recitation of the percussion compositions, using different sounds to imitate the percussion instruments, is konnakol or solkattu. On certain occasions, in a percussion ensemble, one can find a vocal accompanist reciting konnakol or solkattu.

The tala could be technically described as the process of the union (samyoga) and separation (viyoga) of the two hands (palms), in keeping with the ten elements of the unit of musical time which are known as tala dasha pranas (dasha means ten, prana means life). In other words, these are the ten elements that give 'life' to the talas. They are as follows:

1. Kala
2. Kriya
3. Marga
4. Anga
5. Jati
6. Laya
7. Graha
8. Kalai
9. Yati
10. Prastara

1. Kala: This is the very first prana or element of tala which deals with the duration of the angas of the tala. For example, the duration of two anudrutams is equal to one drutam.
2. Kriya: It deals with the different hand gestures used to show the different angas of the talas to count time. This is done by (a) ghata or clap (b) usi or wave, and (c) finger counts. For example, ghata is used for anudrutam, ghata and usi are used for drutam,

and ghata and finger counts are used for the laghu. Kriya can be broadly divided into marga and desi kriyas which are, in turn, divided into (1) sashabda kriya and (2) nisshabda kriya. Sashabda kriya means a kriya which has a sound (like the clap) and nisshabda kriya is one that is silent (like the wave).

3. Marga: The term marga means path or method in Sanskrit. It deals with the duration of kriya in terms of aksharakalas (units of time). It indicates how the kriyas are rhythmically structured in relation to the units of time (aksharas). There are six margas in number:

TABLE 5.7

Margas	*No. of Aksharas*	*No. of Matras*
Dakshina	32	8
Vartika	16	4
Chitra	8	2
Chitratara	4	1
Chitratama	2	½
Ati Chitratama	1	¼

(Each matra is equal to four aksharas)

4. Anga: As explained before, anga literally means limb or part. It is a component of a tala. There are six different angas:
   a. Anudrutam
   b. Drutam
   c. Laghu
   d. Guru
   e. Plutam
   f. Kakapadam

   The first three are the only angas that are used in the seven basic talas. The other three angas were used in the old system of one hundred and eight talas.

a. The anudrutam consists of a clap (shabda kriya—ghata).
b. The drutam consists of a clap and a wave (shabda kriya—ghata and nisshabda kriya—usi).
c. The laghu consists of a clap and finger counts (shabda kriya—ghata and nisshabda kriyas).
d. The guru is equivalent to two chatusra jati laghus. It is a beat followed by a circular clockwise motion of the fist. The guru consists of a total of eight beats.
e. The plutam is equivalent to three chatusra jati laghus with three movements of the hand. The first is a beat, the second is a wave of the hand to the person's left, and the third is a wave to the right. Each movement consists of four beats or aksharas, making it a total of twelve beats.
f. The kakapadam is equivalent to four chatusra jati laghus with four movements of the hand. The first is a beat, the second is an upward wave, the third is a wave to the left and the fourth is a wave to the right side. Each movement consists of four beats or aksharas, making it a total of sixteen beats.

As mentioned earlier, only the first three angas appear in the thirty-five-tala system and the laghu in this system has five jatis or types. The one hundred and eight-tala system uses all the six angas and the laghu used there is constant, consisting of four beats (chatusra jati). Hence, the two units used to describe the time measure are:

1. Akshara, equivalent to one unit, which in turn equals the anudrutam
2. Matra, equivalent to four aksharas (chatusra jati)

The six angas are further expanded into sixteen angas (known as shodasangas, shodasa meaning sixteen) by combinations of the six to give rise to aksharas ranging from one to sixteen.

TABLE 5.8

	Angas	*Symbol*	*Akshara*	*Matra*
1.	Anudrutam (Virama)	◡	1	¼
2.	Drutam	0	2	½
3.	Druta Virama	◡0	3	¾
4.	Laghu (Chatusra Jati)	|	4	1
5.	Laghu Virama	◡|	5	1¼
6.	Laghu Drutam	0|	6	1½
7.	Laghu Druta Virama	◡0|	7	1¾
8.	Guru	8	8	2
9.	Guru Virama	◡8	9	2¼
10.	Guru Drutam	08	10	2½
11.	Guru Druta Virama	◡08	11	2¾
12.	Plutam	|8	12	3
13.	Pluta Virama	◡|8	13	3¼
14.	Pluta Druta	0|8	14	3½
15.	Pluta Druta Virama	◡0|8	15	3¾
16.	Kakapadam	+	16	4

5. Jati: This refers to the type of laghu. As mentioned before, there are five jatis of laghus: tisra jati, chatusra jati, khanda jati, misra jati and sankirna jati.
6. Laya: This is the tempo of the rhythmic cycle. It deals with the time interval between two successive kriyas or aksharas.

Basically, there are three kinds of layas: (1) vilamba laya, or slow, (2) madhya laya or medium, and (3) druta laya or fast. The kriyas in the druta laya are twice as fast as those in the madhya laya, and the kriyas in madhya laya are twice as fast as those in the vilamba laya.

7. Graha: This is the point of the tala cycle where the composition starts. There are two kinds of grahas:
   1. Sama graha (sama means even in Sanskrit)
   2. Vishama graha (vishama means uneven, odd or irregular).

   When the starting point of the compositions falls on the beginning or the first beat (downbeat) of the tala cycle, it is called sama graha. When it does not fall on the first beat, it is called vishama graha. Vishama graha is further subdivided into two kinds:

   a. Ateeta graha (starting before the downbeat)
   b. Anagata graha (starting after the downbeat)

   When the composition starts before the sama or downbeat of the cycle, it is known as ateeta graha and when it starts after the sama, it is called anagata graha.

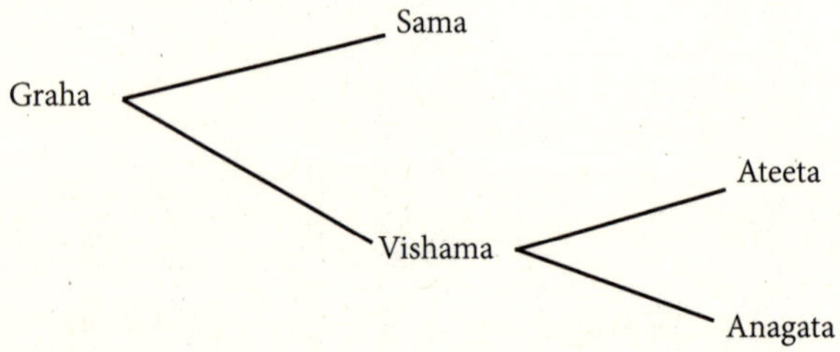

8. Kala (kalai): It refers to the subdivision of each unit (kriya) of the tala cycle. For example, eka kalai or one kalai is where there is only one swara or note for each kriya of the tala. Dvikala or two kalais is where there are two subdivisions for each kriya. Chatush kalai or four kalais is where there are four subdivisions.

9. Yati: This element deals with the order of arrangements of different angas in a tala cycle. There are six kinds of yatis. All the six yatis are applicable to the one hundred and eight-tala system, whereas not all of them apply to the thirty-five-tala system.

(a) Sama yati: where the angas are all uniform or of the same kind, for example:

(i) Udgbatta tala has three gurus 888

(ii) Shat tala has six drutams 000000

(b) Gopuchcha ('Cow's Tail') yati: the angas with a higher number of beats appear in the beginning followed by angas with a lesser number of beats (in diminishing order, like a cow's tail), for example:

(i) Sama tala | |00 ◡

(ii) Utsava tala $\overset{|}{8}$|

(c) Srotovaha yati: where it is the reverse of gopuchcha yati-angas of a lesser number of beats appear in the beginning followed by angas of a higher number of beats, for example:

(i) Tribhinna tala |8 $\overset{|}{8}$

(ii) Rati tala |8

(iii) Rupaka tala (from the thirty-five-tala scheme) 0|

(d) Damaru yati: where the angas are arranged so that they are narrow in the centre and broader towards the extremities. This resembles the percussion instrument, the damaru, which Shiva has in his hand, for example:

(i) Dhenkika tala 8|8

(ii) Matyu tala (from the thirty-five-tala scheme) |0|

(e) Mridanga yati: where angas are broadest at the centre and diminish towards the extremities. This resembles the shape of the mridangam—hence the name, for example:

(i) Dvitiya tala 0|0

(ii) Pratimatya tala | |88| |

(f) Vishama yati: where the angas are in an irregular order, for example:

(i)	Vilokita tala	$|800\,\overset{|}{8}$
(ii)	Chaturmukha tala	$|8|\overset{|}{8}$
(iii)	Jhamba tala (from the thirty-five-tala scheme)	$|\smile 0$

10. Prastara: This final element is purely of theoretical interest. Prastara literally means 'spreading out' or 'elaborating'. Prastara of a particular anga means substituting that anga with other possible permutations and combinations of angas to give the same number of kriyas. For example, for the tisra laghu $|_3$ (three beats), the prastaras are:

(i)	Drutasekharam	$\overset{\smile}{0} = 3$ beats
(ii)	Drutam and anudrutam	$0\smile = 2 + 1 = 3$ beats
(iii)	Anudrutam and drutam	$\smile 0 = 1 + 2 = 3$ beats
(iv)	Three Anudrutams	$\smile\smile\smile = 1 + 1 + 1 = 3$ beats

Chapu Talas

Beside the ancient system of the hundred and eight talas and the system of 175 talas in current use, there is another group of talas, the chapu talas. These have been used in Indian music from very early times. A lot of folk melodies are based on this rhythmic structure. They are syncopated rhythmic cycles. There are four types of chapu talas:

1. Tisra chapu, consisting of three beats, which could be divided 1+2;
2. Khanda chapu, consisting of five beats, which could be divided 2+3;
3. Misra chapu, consisting of seven beats, which could be divided 3+2+2 (or 2+2+3);
4. Sankirna chapu, consisting of nine beats, which could be divided 2+2+2+3.

Of these, the most commonly used are misra chapu and khanda chapu. When no specific type of chapu is mentioned and the tala merely says 'chapu tala', it is presumed to be misra chapu tala. Many great composers have written compositions in this group of talas which are still commonly used today. The specific factors that apply to these talas are:

(i) each unit is one beat and these beats are never further subdivided into smaller units. In other words, the dasa prana element of kalai does not apply here.
(ii) these tala cycles are generally faster in tempo than the thirty-five-tala cycles.

Desadi and Madhyadi Talas

These are four-beat cycles starting with a wave of the hand up in the air (visarjita) followed by three beats. The desadi tala is in a slower tempo than the madhyadi tala. In the desadi tala, the composition starts in the visarjita after three-fourths of a beat. In the madhyadi tala, the composition starts after half a beat. In both, there is a silence, or rest (visranti) at the beginning of the tala cycle. These are believed to have come into Carnatic music practice during the time of the great composer Tyagaraja.

The above groups of rhythmic cycles form the bulk of the talas that are currently used in south Indian classical music. Besides these, there are also some complicated rhythmic cycles that are used in a musical form called Tiruppugazh, created by the saint-poet Arunagirinathar. With all the possible complex rhythmic cycles and with the freedom that the performer has in the Carnatic tradition, it is impossible to describe the extent of the complexities of rhythmic structure and patterns that some performers have devised, still staying within the strict framework of the tradition.

There are also pallavis where compositions have been created and performed in all the five nadais within one cycle of tala and elaborated with improvisations like neraval and swara-kalpana (see the explanation of ragam-tanam-pallavi under Musical Forms). Also, there are cases where performers take compositions, like varnams and complex pallavis, and play them in multiple speeds in the different nadais. This is very complex rhythmically because it involves taking a composition which is written, for example, in an eight-beat cycle where each beat is divided into four pulses per beat (chatusra nadai), and performing it, for example, in khanda or misra nadai (five or seven pulses per beat). When this is done, the whole phrasing of the composition changes and falls in totally different places in the rhythmic cycle. In order to bring the composition back to its original starting point or eduppu, one has to repeat certain lines more than once. As one goes into the higher speeds in different nadais, it becomes a challenge to one's musicianship and virtuosity to accomplish this, keeping the aesthetic value alive in the music.

It is also customary during improvisations based on the sol-fa syllables (swara kalpana), to form a rhythmic pattern and repeat it three times to come back to the starting point of the composition. These rhythmic patterns could get extremely complicated, technically and musically, depending on the performer's creativity and skills in incorporating all the different nadais and tempi in these patterns. Because of the immense scope of improvisation and the creative genius of some great artists, the rhythmic concepts have been taken to greater and greater heights. One has to listen and understand to believe it.

INTRODUCTION TO BASIC NORTH INDIAN TALAS

In north Indian classical music, tabla is typically the accompanying percussion instrument. The left-hand drum of the tabla is known as the 'bayan' and the right-hand drum is known as the 'tabla'.

The following are the principal 'gharanas' or schools of tabla-playing—Delhi, Benaras, Punjab, Ajrada, Lucknow and Farukhabad.

There are separate time cycles used for vocal and instrumental music.

For vocal music the most popular talas are –

Ektal

12 beats

Theka:

+					
Dhin	Dhin	Dhage	Terekete	Thun	Na
1	2	0		2	
		3	4	5	6

Kat	Ta	Dhage	Terekete	Dhin	Dhadha
0		3		4	
7	8	9	10	11	12
					(+) Dhin

Tilwada

16 beats

Theka :

Dha	Terekete	Dhin	Aa Dha	Dha	Dhage	Tin	Tin
1	2	3	4	5	6	7	8

Ta	Terekete	Dhin	Aa Dha	Dha	Dhage	Dhin	Dhadha
8	9	11	12	13	14	15	16

Jhumra

14 beats

Theka:

Dhin	Dhage	Terekete	Dhin	Dhin	Dhage	Terekete
1	2	3	4	5	6	7

Tin	Take	Terekete	Dhin	Dhin	Dhage	Terekete
8	9	10	11	12	13	14
						(+) Dhin

The slower tempo exposition of the tala is known as vilambit.

This is a concept of stretching a beat into different micro-beats. For example,

Ektal – 24 beats
Medium tempo / 1 beat = 2 micro beats

Dhin	=	Dhin	=	Dha	Dha Dhaga	Tere	Kete
1	2	3	4	5	6	7	8
Thun	=	Na	Na na	Kat	=	Ta	=
9	10	11	12	13	14	15	16
Dha	Dhage	Tere	Kete	Dhin	=	Dha	Dha
17	18	19	20	21	22	23	24

Ektal – 48 beats
Medium tempo / 1 beat = 4 micro beats

Dhin	=	=	=	Dhin	=	=	=	Dha	=	=	Dhage	Te	Re	Ke	Te
1	2	3	4	5	6	7	8	9	10	11	12	13	14	15	16
Thun	=	=	=	Na	=	Na	Na	Kat	=	=	Teta	Ta	=	=	Teta
17	18	19	20	21	22	23	24	25	26	27	28	29	30	31	32
Dha	=	=	Dhage	Te	re	ke	te	Dhin	=	=	Credhin Tat	Dha	=	Dha	Dhadha
33	34	35	36	37	38	39	40	41	42	43	44	45	46	47	48

Jhumra – 56 beats
Medium tempo / 1 beat = 4 micro beats

Dhin	=	=	=	Dha	=	=	Dhage	Te	Re	Ke	Te
1	2	3	4	5	6	7	8	9	10	11	12
Dhin	=	=	=	Dhin	=	=	=	Dha	=	=	Dhage
13	14	15	16	17	18	19	20	21	22	23	24
Te	Re	Ke	Te	Tin	=	=	=	Te	=	=	Take
25	26	27	28	29	30	31	32	33	34	35	36

Te	Re	Ke	Te	Dhin	=	=	=	Dhin	=	=	=
37	38	39	40	41	42	43	44	45	46	47	48

Dha	=	=	Dhage	Te	Re	Ke	Te	+
49	50	51	52	53	54	55	56	(Dhin)

To understand the division of a particular tala, we have to take into consideration the system of counting the beats or matras with definite hand gestures.

The two most important features of the tala system are the 'sam' (first beat with a clap) and the 'khali' (an open hand movement). They are depicted as follows –

+ for Sam

O for Khali

The others most important factor of accompaniment is 'amaad' which refers to the different patterns that a demonstrator should display to reach the sam or the starting matra of any composition.

	+						
Taki	Tedha	Kata	Dha	Taki	Tedha	Kata	Dha
1	2	3	4	5	6	7	8
Taki	Tedka	Kata	Dha	Taki	Tedha	Kata	Dha
9	10	11	12	13	14	15	16

| • Bandish starting point

To develop a sense of rhythm it is important to recite the tala with definite hand gestures. It is advisable to try and play the theka and simultaneously recite the syllables. Regular recitation and practice can help develop clear pronunciation.

Important talas for solo and accompaniment include the following –

Ektal

12 beats

+							
Dhin	Dhin	Dhage	Terekete	Thun	Na	Kat	Ta
		0		2		0	
1	2	3	4	5	6	7	8

Dhage	Terekete	Dhin	Dhadha	+ (Dhin)
3		4		
9	10	11	12	1

Teental

16 beats

+							
Dha	Dhin	Dhin	Dha	Dha	Dhin	Dhin	Dha
				2			
1	2	3	4	5	6	7	8

								+
Dha	Tin	Tin	Ta	Na	Dhin	Dhin	Dha	(Dha)
0				3				
9	10	11	12	13	14	15	16	1

Jhaptal

10 beats

+						
Dhin	Na	Dhin	Dhin	Na	Tin	Na
		2			0	
1	2	3	4	5	6	7

+			
Dhin	Dhin	Na	(Dhin)
3			1
8	9	10	

Rupak

7 beats

This tala starts from khali (open hand movement).

Tin	Tin	Na	Dhin	Na	Dhin	Na	(Tin)
0			1		2		0
1	2	3	4	5	6	7	

Ada Chautal

14 beats

+							
Dhin	Terekete	Dhin	Na	Thun	Na	Kat	Ta
		2		0		3	
1	2	3	4	5	6	7	8

Terekete	Dhin	Na	Dhin	Dhin	Na	(Dhin)
0		4		o		1
9	10	11	12	13	14	

Dadra

6 beats

+						
Dha	Dhin	Na	Na	Tin	Na	(Dha)
			0			
1	2	3	4	5	6	1

Keherwa

8 beats

+								+
Dha	Ga	Te	Te	Na	Ga	Dhin	Na	(Dha)
				0				1
=	2	3	4	5	6	7	8	

6

Comparison between Carnatic (South Indian) and Hindustani (North Indian) Music

Carnatic and Hindustani traditions have the same roots and developed along the same lines until about the twelfth century CE, when music in the north began developing along different lines due to foreign influences.

Fundamentally, the two systems are similar in raga and tala conceptualisation and in the use of swara and shruti. However, it is the different style of rendering notes, ornamentations, treatment of ragas and a vast difference in the rhythmic concepts that give each system its distinctive colour. Relatively speaking, Carnatic music may be said to be more systematised than Hindustani music.

REGIONS

Carnatic music is the tradition of the southern states in India: Tamil Nadu, Karnataka, Kerala, Telangana and Andhra Pradesh. Hindustani music is prevalent in the other states of India. The language used commonly in Hindustani classical music is Hindi (and its dialectal Braj Bhasha), whereas the languages used in Carnatic music are Sanskrit, Telugu, Tamil and Kannada.

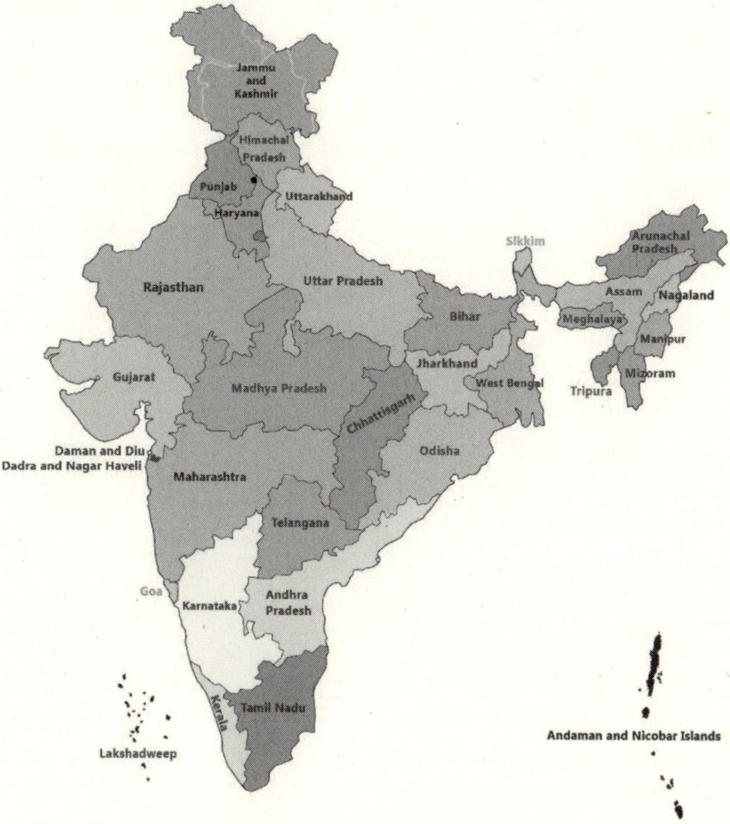

PARENT AND DERIVED SCALES

Both systems have parent scales from which other scales are derived. The South follows the system of seventy-two parent scales (called melakartas) as devised by the great scholar Venkatamakhi in the seventeenth century. The north follows a system of ten basic parent scales (known as thaats) as devised by the scholar V.N. Bhatkhande in the early twentieth century. Bhatkhande drew upon the seventy-two parent scales of Venkatamakhi and selected only ten of them which could be, according to him, conveniently used for Hindustani ragas.

Here is a brief overview of the seventy-two Melakarta System of south Indian classical music.

The basic seven-note system is further divided into twelve semitones. Using the principle of enharmonics, we get a total of sixteen notes in south Indian classical music, which are designated as follows:

S = Tonic

R_1 = Minor second

R_2 = Major second

R_3 = Augmented second

G_1 = Diminished third

G_2 = Minor third

G_3 = Major third

M_1 = Perfect fourth

M_2 = Augmented fourth

P = Perfect fifth

D_1 = Minor sixth

D_2 = Major sixth

D_3 = Augmented sixth

N_1 = Diminished seventh

N_2 = Minor seventh

N_3 = Major seventh

[Note: $R_2 = G_1$, $R_3 = G_2$, $D_2 = N_1$, and $D_3 = N_2$.]

The seventy-two melakartas are divided into twelve groups known as Chakras—Indu, Nethra, Agni, Veda, Bana, Rutu, Rishi, Vasu, Brahma, Dishi, Rudra, and Aditya.

I. Indu Chakra

1. Kanakangi S R_1 G_1 M_1 P D_1 N_1 $\dot{S}$ — $\dot{S}$ N_1 D_1 P M_1 G_1 R_1 S
2. Ratnangi S R_1 G_1 M_1 P D_1 N_2 $\dot{S}$ — $\dot{S}$ N_2 D_1 P M_1 G_1 R_1 S

3. Ganamurti S R_1 G_1 M_1 P D_1 N_3 $\dot{S}$ — $\dot{S}$ N_3 D_1 P M_1 G_1 R_1 S
4. Vanaspati S R_1 G_1 M_1 P D_2 N_2 $\dot{S}$ — $\dot{S}$ N_2 D_2 P M_1 G_1 R_1 S
5. Manavati S R_1 G_1 M_1 P D_2 N_3 $\dot{S}$ — $\dot{S}$ N_3 D_2 P M_1 G_1 R_1 S
6. Tanarupi S R_1 G_1 M_1 P D_3 N_3 $\dot{S}$ — $\dot{S}$ N_3 D_3 P M_1 G_1 R_1 S

II. Netra Chakra

7. Senavati $S\ R_1\ G_2\ M_1\ P\ D_1\ N_1\ \dot{S}$ — $\dot{S}\ N_1\ D_1\ P\ M_1\ G_2\ R_1\ S$
8. Hanumatodi $S\ R_1\ G_2\ M_1\ P\ D_1\ N_2\ \dot{S}$ — $\dot{S}\ N_2\ D_1\ P\ M_1\ G_2\ R_1\ S$
9. Dhenuka $S\ R_1\ G_2\ M_1\ P\ D_1\ N_3\ \dot{S}$ — $\dot{S}\ N_3\ D_1\ P\ M_1\ G_2\ R_1\ S$
10. Natakapriya $S\ R_1\ G_2\ M_1\ P\ D_2\ N_2\ \dot{S}$ — $\dot{S}\ N_2\ D_2\ P\ M_1\ G_2\ R_1\ S$
11. Kokilapriya $S\ R_1\ G_2\ M_1\ P\ D_2\ N_3\ \dot{S}$ — $\dot{S}\ N_3\ D_2\ P\ M_1\ G_2\ R_1\ S$
12. Rupavati $S\ R_1\ G_2\ M_1\ P\ D_3\ N_3\ \dot{S}$ — $\dot{S}\ N_3\ D_3\ P\ M_1\ G_2\ R_1\ S$

III. Agni Chakra

13. Gayakapriya $S\ R_1\ G_3\ M_1\ P\ D_1\ N_1\ \dot{S}$ — $\dot{S}\ N_1\ D_1\ P\ M_1\ G_3\ R_1\ S$
14. Vakulabharanam $S\ R_1\ G_3\ M_1\ P\ D_1\ N_2\ \dot{S}$ — $\dot{S}\ N_2\ D_1\ P\ M_1\ G_3\ R_1\ S$
15. Mayamalavagowla $S\ R_1\ G_3\ M_1\ P\ D_1\ N_3\ \dot{S}$ — $\dot{S}\ N_3\ D_1\ P\ M_1\ G_3\ R_1\ S$
16. Chakravakam $S\ R_1\ G_3\ M_1\ P\ D_2\ N_2\ \dot{S}$ — $\dot{S}\ N_2\ D_2\ P\ M_1\ G_3\ R_1\ S$
17. Suryakantam $S\ R_1\ G_3\ M_1\ P\ D_2\ N_3\ \dot{S}$ — $\dot{S}\ N_3\ D_2\ P\ M_1\ G_3\ R_1\ S$
18. Hatakambari $S\ R_1\ G_3\ M_1\ P\ D_3\ N_3\ \dot{S}$ — $\dot{S}\ N_3\ D_3\ P\ M_1\ G_3\ R_1\ S$

IV. Veda Chakra

19. Jhankaradhwani $S\ R_2\ G_2\ M_1\ P\ D_1\ N_1\ \dot{S}$ — $\dot{S}\ Nv\ D_1\ P\ M_1\ G_2\ R_2\ S$
20. Natabhairavi $S\ R_2\ G_2\ M_1\ P\ D_1\ N_2\ \dot{S}$ — $\dot{S}\ N_2\ D_1\ P\ M_1\ G_2\ R_2\ S$
21. Kiravani $S\ R_2\ G_2\ M_1\ P\ D_1\ N_3\ \dot{S}$ — $\dot{S}\ N_3\ D_1\ P\ M_1\ G_2\ R_2\ S$
22. Kharaharapriya $S\ R_2\ G_2\ M_1\ P\ D_2\ N_2\ \dot{S}$ — $\dot{S}\ N_2\ D_2\ P\ M_1\ G_2\ R_2\ S$
23. Gaurimanohari $S\ R_2\ G_2\ M_1\ P\ D_2\ N_3\ \dot{S}$ — $\dot{S}\ N_3\ D_2\ P\ M_1\ G_2\ R_2\ S$
24. Varunapriya $S\ R_2\ G_2\ M_1\ P\ D_3\ N_3\ \dot{S}$ — $\dot{S}\ N_3\ D_3\ P\ M_1\ G_2\ R_2\ S$

C

13 Gayakapriya

14 Vakulabharanam

15 Mayamalavagaula

16 Chakravakam

17 Suryakantam

18 Hatakambari

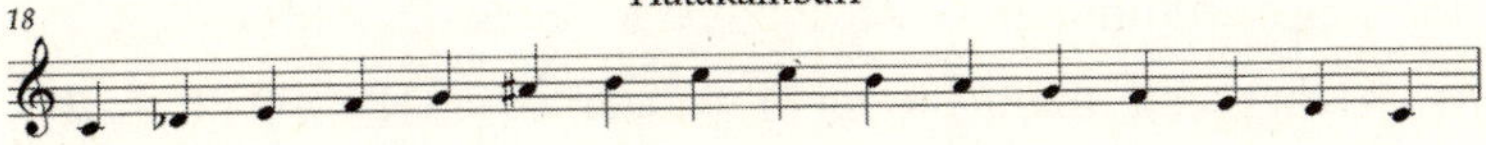

D

19 Jhankaradhvani

20 Natabhairavi

21 Kiravani

22 Kharaharapriya

23 Gourimanohari

24 Varunapriya

V. Bana Chakra

25. Mararanjani S R_2 G_3 M_1 P D_1 N_1 $\dot{S}$ — $\dot{S}$ N_1 D_1 P M_1 G_3 R_2 S
26. Charukesi S R_2 G_3 M_1 P D_1 N_2 $\dot{S}$ — $\dot{S}$ N_2 D_1 P M_1 G_3 R_2 S
27. Sarasangi S R_2 G_3 M_1 P D_1 N_3 $\dot{S}$ — $\dot{S}$ N_3 D_1 P M_1 G_3 R_2 S
28. Harikambhoji S R_2 G_3 M_1 P D_2 N_2 $\dot{S}$ — $\dot{S}$ N_2 D_2 P M_1 G_3 R_2 S
29. Dhirasankarabaranam S R_2 G_3 M_1 P D_2 N_3 $\dot{S}$ — $\dot{S}$ N_3 D_2 P M_1 G_3 R_2 S
30. Naganandini S R_2 G_3 M_1 P D_3 N_3 $\dot{S}$ — $\dot{S}$ N_3 D_3 P M_1 G_3 R_2 S

VI. Rutu Chakra

31. Yagapriya S R_3 G_3 M_1 P D_1 N_1 $\dot{S}$ — $\dot{S}$ N_1 D_1 P M_1 G_3 R_3 S
32. Ragavardhini S R_3 G_3 M_1 P D_1 N_2 $\dot{S}$ — $\dot{S}$ N_2 D_1 P M_1 G_3 R_3 S
33. Gangeyabhushani S R_3 G_3 M_1 P D_1 N_3 $\dot{S}$ — $\dot{S}$ N_3 D_1 P M_1 G_3 R_3 S
34. Vagadheeswari S R_3 G_3 M_1 P D_2 N_2 $\dot{S}$ — $\dot{S}$ N_2 D_2 P M_1 G_3 R_3 S
35. Shulini S R_3 G_3 M_1 P D_2 N_3 $\dot{S}$ — $\dot{S}$ N_3 D_2 P M_1 G_3 R_3 S
36. Chalanata S R_3 G_3 M_1 P D_3 N_3 $\dot{S}$ — $\dot{S}$ N_3 D_3 P M_1 G_3 R_3 S

E

25 Mararanjani

26 Charukesi

27 Sarasangi

28 Harikambhoji

29 Dhirasankarabharanam

30 Naganandini

F

31 Yagapriya

32 Ragavardhani

33 Gangeyabhushani

34 Vagadhisvari

35 Sulini

36 Chalanata

VII. Rishi Chakra

37. Salagam $S\ R_1\ G_1\ M_2\ P\ D_1\ N_1\ \dot{S}$ — $\dot{S}\ N_1\ D_1\ P\ M_2\ G_1\ R_1\ S$
38. Jalarnavam $S\ R_1\ G_1\ M_2\ P\ D_1\ N_2\ \dot{S}$ — $\dot{S}\ N_2\ D_1\ P\ M_2\ G_1\ R_1\ S$
39. Jhalavarali $S\ R_1\ G_1\ M_2\ P\ D_1\ N_3\ \dot{S}$ — $\dot{S}\ N_3\ D_1\ P\ M_2\ G_1\ R_1\ S$
40. Navanitam $S\ R_1\ G_1\ M_2\ P\ D_2\ N_2\ \dot{S}$ — $\dot{S}\ N_2\ D_2\ P\ M_2\ G_1\ R_1\ S$
41. Pavani $S\ R_1\ G_1\ M_2\ P\ D_2\ N_3\ \dot{S}$ — $\dot{S}\ N_3\ D_2\ P\ M_2\ G_1\ R_1\ S$
42. Raghupriya $S\ R_1\ G_1\ M_2\ P\ D_3\ N_3\ \dot{S}$ — $\dot{S}\ N_3\ D_3\ P\ M_2\ G_1\ R_1\ S$

VIII. Vasu Chakra

43. Gavambhodi $S\ R_1\ G_2\ M_2\ P\ D_1\ N_1\ \dot{S}$ — $\dot{S}\ N_1\ D_1\ P\ M_2\ G_2\ R_1\ S$
44. Bhavapriya $S\ R_1\ G_2\ M_2\ P\ D_1\ N_2\ \dot{S}$ — $\dot{S}\ N_2\ D_1\ P\ M_2\ G_2\ R_1\ S$
45. Shubhapantuvarali $S\ R_1\ G_2\ M_2\ P\ D_1\ N_3\ \dot{S}$ — $\dot{S}\ N_3\ D_1\ P\ M_2\ G_2\ R_1\ S$
46. Shadvidamargini $S\ R_1\ G_2\ M_2\ P\ D_2\ N_2\ \dot{S}$ — $\dot{S}\ N_2\ D_2\ P\ M_2\ G_2\ R_1\ S$
47. Suvarnangi $S\ R_1\ G_2\ M_2\ P\ D_2\ N_3\ \dot{S}$ — $\dot{S}\ N_3\ D_2\ P\ M_2\ G_2\ R_1\ S$
48. Divyamani $S\ R_1\ G_2\ M_2\ P\ D_3\ N_3\ \dot{S}$ — $\dot{S}\ N_3\ D_3\ P\ M_2\ G_2\ R_1\ S$

G

Salagam

37

Jalarnavam

38

Jhalavarali

39

Navanitam

40

Pavani

41

Raghupriya

42
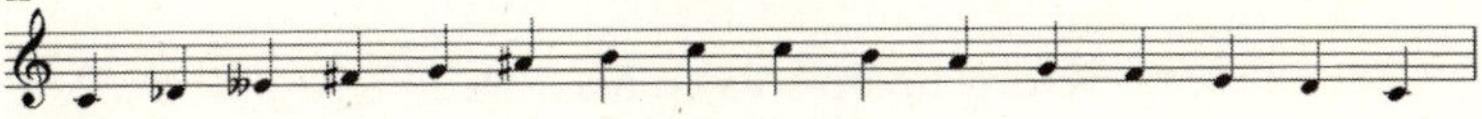

H

Gavambhodi

43

Bhavapriya

44

Subhapantuvarali

45

Shadvidhamargini

46

Suvarnangi

47

Divyamani

48

IX. Brahma Chakra

49. Dhavalambari S R_1 G_3 M_2 P D_1 N_1 $\dot{S}$ — $\dot{S}$ N_1 D_1 P M_2 G_3 R_1 S
50. Namanarayani S R_1 G_3 M_2 P D_1 N_2 $\dot{S}$ — $\dot{S}$ N_2 D_1 P M_2 G_3 R_1 S
51. Kamavardhini S R_1 G_3 M_2 P D_1 N_3 $\dot{S}$ — $\dot{S}$ N_3 D_1 P M_2 G_3 R_1 S
52. Ramapriya S R_1 G_3 M_2 P D_2 N_2 $\dot{S}$ — $\dot{S}$ N_2 D_2 P M_2 G_3 R_1 S
53. Gamanasrama S R_1 G_3 M_2 P D_2 N_3 $\dot{S}$ — $\dot{S}$ N_3 D_2 P M_2 G_3 R_1 S
54. Vishvambari S R_1 G_3 M_2 P D_3 N_3 $\dot{S}$ — $\dot{S}$ N_3 D_3 P M_2 G_3 R_1 S

X. Dishi Chakra

55. Syamalangi S R_2 G_2 M_2 P D_1 N_1 $\dot{S}$ — $\dot{S}$ N_1 D_1 P M_2 G_2 R_2 S
56. Shanmukhapriya S R_2 G_2 M_2 P D_1 N_2 $\dot{S}$ — $\dot{S}$ N_2 D_1 P M_2 G_2 R_2 S
57. Simhendra-Madhyamam S R_2 G_2 M_2 P D_1 N_3 $\dot{S}$ — $\dot{S}$ N_3 D_1 P M_2 G_2 R_2 S
58. Hemavati S R_2 G_2 M_2 P D_2 N_2 $\dot{S}$ — $\dot{S}$ N_2 D_2 P M_2 G_2 R_2 S
59. Dharmavati S R_2 G_2 M_2 P D_2 N_3 $\dot{S}$ — $\dot{S}$ N_3 D_2 P M_2 G_2 R_2 S
60. Nitimati S R_2 G_2 M_2 P D_3 N_3 $\dot{S}$ — $\dot{S}$ N_3 D_3 P M_2 G_2 R_2 S

I

49 Dhavalambari

50 Namanarayani

51 Kamavardhini

52 Ramapriya

53 Gamanasrama

54 Vishvambari

J

55 Syamalangi

56 Shanmukhapriya

57 Simhendra Madhyaman

58 Hemavati

59 Dharmavati

60 Nitimati

XI. Rudra Chakra

61. Kantamani $S\ R_2\ G_3\ M_2\ P\ D_1\ N_1\ \dot{S}$ — $\dot{S}\ N_1\ D_1\ P\ M_2\ G_3\ R_2\ S$

62. Rishabhapriya $S\ R_2\ G_3\ M_2\ P\ D_1\ N_2\ \dot{S}$ — $\dot{S}\ N_2\ D_1\ P\ M_2\ G_3\ R_2\ S$

63. Latangi $S\ R_2\ G_3\ M_2\ P\ D_1\ N_3\ \dot{S}$ — $\dot{S}\ N_3\ D_1\ P\ M_2\ G_3\ R_2\ S$

64. Vachaspati $S\ R_2\ G_3\ M_2\ P\ D_2\ N_2\ \dot{S}$ — $\dot{S}\ N_2\ D_2\ P\ M_2\ G_3\ R_2\ S$

65. Mechakalyani $S\ R_2\ G_3\ M_2\ P\ D_2\ N_3\ \dot{S}$ — $\dot{S}\ N_3\ D_2\ P\ M_2\ G_3\ R_2\ S$

66. Chitrambari $S\ R_2\ G_3\ M_2\ P\ D_3\ N_3\ \dot{S}$ — $\dot{S}\ N_3\ D_3\ P\ M_2\ G_3\ R_2\ S$

XII. Aditya Chakra

67. Sucharitra $S\ R_3\ G_3\ M_2\ P\ D_1\ N_1\ \dot{S}$ — $\dot{S}\ N_1\ D_1\ P\ M_2\ G_3\ R_3\ S$

68. Jyotisvarupini $S\ R_3\ G_3\ M_2\ P\ D_1\ N_2\ \dot{S}$ — $\dot{S}\ N_2\ D_1\ P\ M_2\ G_3\ R_3\ S$

69. Dhatuvardani $S\ R_3\ G_3\ M_2\ P\ D_1\ N_3\ \dot{S}$ — $\dot{S}\ N_3\ D_1\ P\ M_2\ G_3\ R_3\ S$

70. Nasikabhushani $S\ R_3\ G_3\ M_2\ P\ D_2\ N_2\ \dot{S}$ — $\dot{S}\ N_2\ D_2\ P\ M_2\ G_3\ R_3\ S$

71. Kosalam $S\ R_3\ G_3\ M_2\ P\ D_2\ N_3\ \dot{S}$ — $\dot{S}\ N_3\ D_2\ P\ M_2\ G_3\ R_3\ S$

72. Rasikapriya $S\ R_3\ G_3\ M_2\ P\ D_3\ N_3\ \dot{S}$ — $\dot{S}\ N_3\ D_3\ P\ M_2\ G_3\ R_3\ S$

K
61
Kantamani
62
Rishabhapriya
63
Latangi
64
Vachaspati
65
Mechakalyani
66
Chitrambari
L
67
Sucharitra
68
Jyothisvarupini
69
Dhatuvardhani
70
Nasikabhushani
71
Kosalam
72
Rasikapriya

The graphical representation of first melakarta of each chakra is given below –

Indu Chakra / Mela 1 / Kanakangi

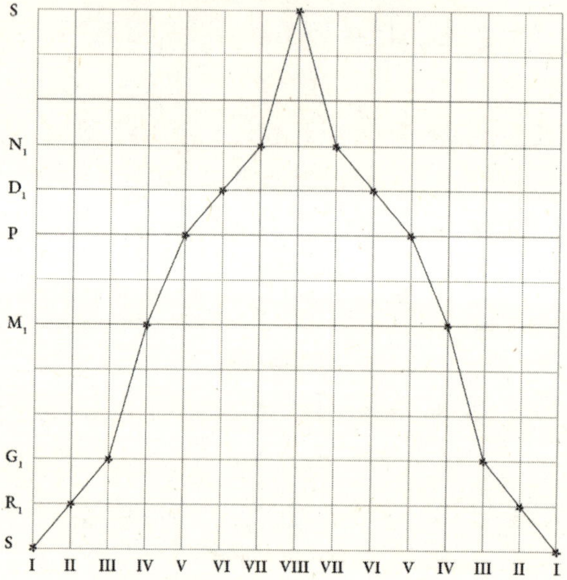

Agni Chakra / Mela 13 / Gayakapriya

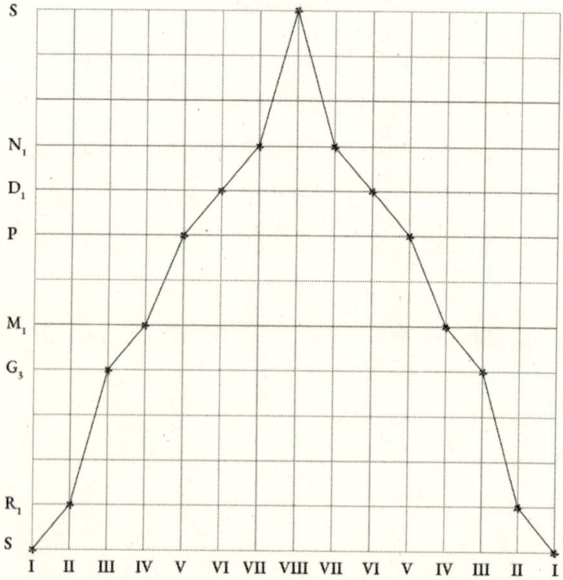

Veda Chakra / Mela 19 / Jhankaradhvani

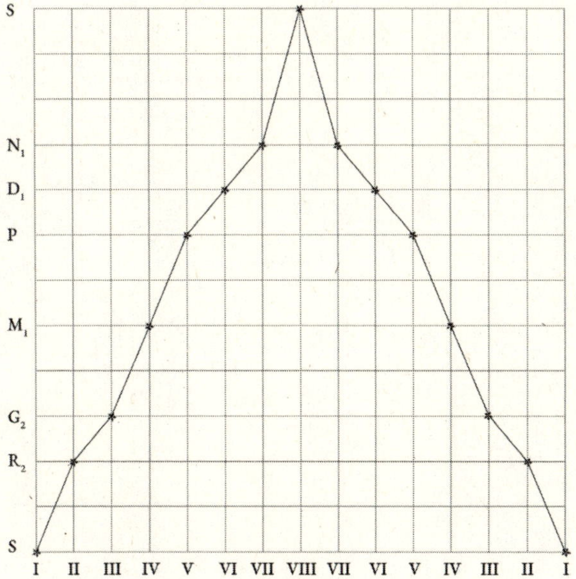

Bana Chakra / Mela 25 / Mararanjani

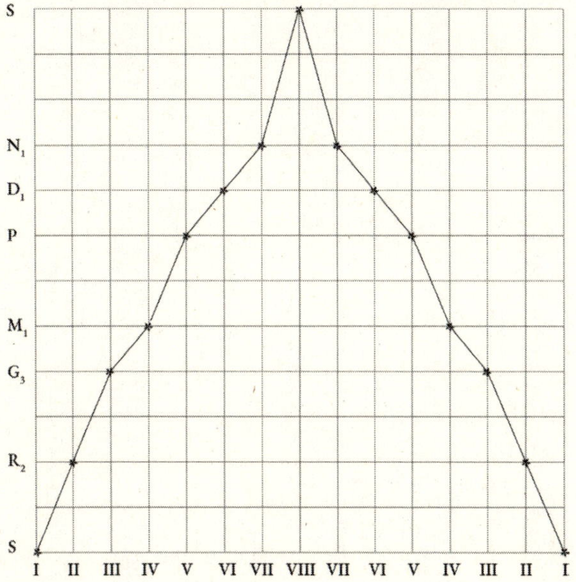

Rutu Chakra / Mela 31 / Yagapriya

Rishi Chakra / Mela 37 / Salagam

Vasu Chakra / Mela 43 / Gavambodhi

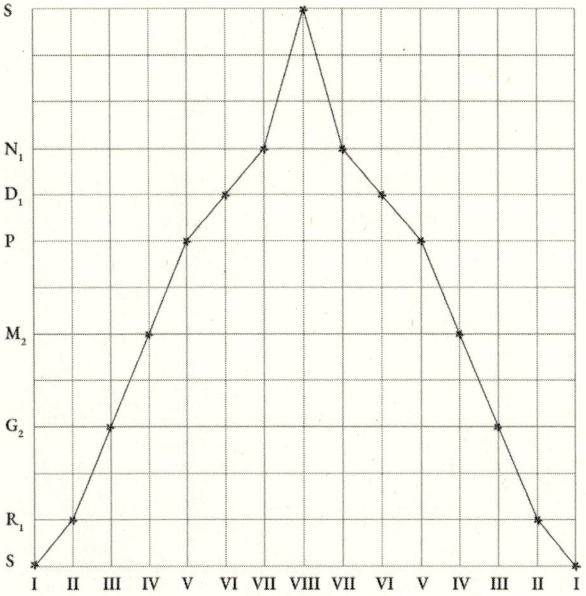

Brahma Chakra / Mela 49 / Dhavalambari

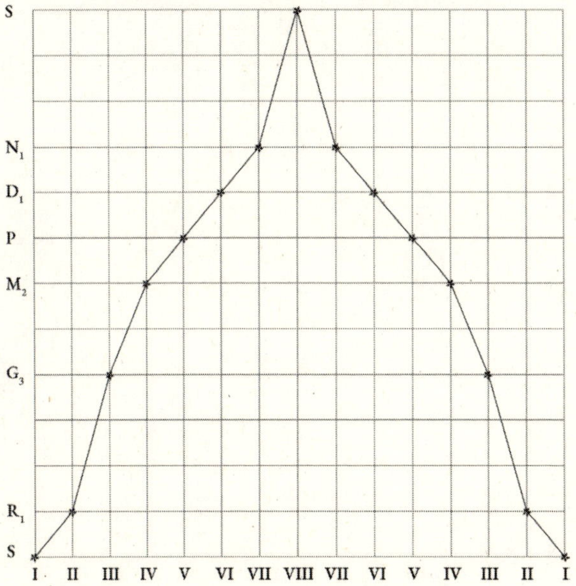

Dishi Chakra / Mela 55 / Syamalangi

Rudra Chakra / Mela 61 / Kantamani

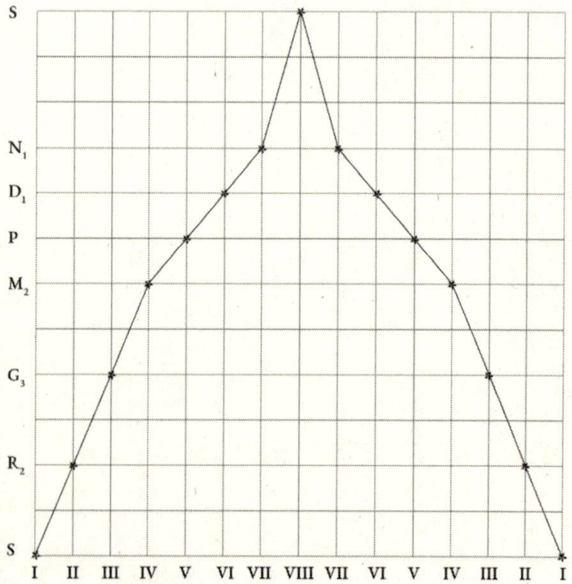

Aditya Chakra / Mela 67 / Sucharitra

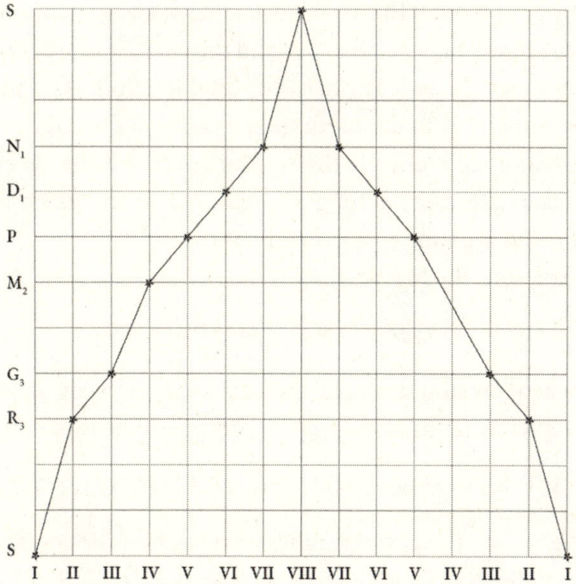

The seventy-two melakartas can be played in each of the twelve semitones, giving a total of eight hundred and sixty-four scales in south Indian classical music. Traditionally, the scales of the melakarta ragas have the same notes in the arohana (ascent) and avarohana (descent), following the same sequence. If we were to change this and have different arohanas and avarohanas, that increases the number of possibilities and we get a total of five thousand one hundred and eighty-four scales from the seventy-two basic scales. Playing those in the twelve different positions, we get sixty-two thousand two hundred and eight basic scales.

If we go to derived scales by omitting certain notes from the parent scale (varjya), or creating a zigzag pattern in the arohana and avarohana (vakra), introducing one or more foreign notes (bhashanga), and a combination of any of these. In this manner, we can definitely get more than a million scales in south Indian classical music.

Bhatkhande has classified all the north Indian ragas under one or the other of the ten thaats, the principle of classification adopted being the affinity between the raga and the janak thaat (parent scale) to which it was allotted. The derived scales in Hindustani music are not as systematic as in the south Indian classical system.

One major difference is that in the South, all the seventy-two parent scales can also be sung as ragas, but in the north only the derived scales are sung as ragas and not the thaats.

For example, the Marwa thaat is

$$S\ r\ G\ M\ P\ D\ N\ \dot{S} - \dot{S}\ N\ D\ P\ M\ G\ r\ S$$

but when it is sung as a raga, the Sa is used very sparingly and the Pa is completely omitted; the raga usually goes like this:

D N r G M D N D; D M G r; r G M D N r; r N D M G r G r N D; D N r S

In the South, the corresponding melakarta, Gamanasrama, has the same notes: $S\ R_1\ G_3\ M_2\ P\ D_2\ N_3\ \dot{S} - \dot{S}\ N_3\ D_2\ P\ M_2\ G_3\ R_1\ S$ and when this is sung as a raga, it uses all the seven notes.

The eminent south Indian composer Tyagaraja is said to have written compositions in about two hundred and fifty ragas, which is probably the most any composer has written. In the north, there are much fewer ragas in regular use.

TIME THEORY

The north of India follows the time theory of ragas, which states that every raga can be performed only at a specific time of the day or night. The ragas are divided into purva and uttara ragas. Purva ragas are those that are typically performed in the first half of the day and uttara ragas are those that are sung or played in the second half. Also known as purvanga-vadi ragas, the purva ragas are those that have the vadi in the first half of the scale or the first tetra chord, and the uttara or uttaranga-vadi ragas have the vadi note in the second half or the second tetra chord. Additionally, different ragas are associated with different seasons; for instance, ragas from the Malhar family for the monsoons, Basant for the spring, etc. In South India, this time theory is not followed, although there are ragas linked with particular times of the day: for instance, Bhoopalam and Gaula for the early morning, Bilahari and Malahari for the late morning, and Madhyamavati and Sri Raga for midday. However, since these ragas are also performed at other times of the day, the performer is not limited to a lesser number of ragas. In the north, due to this restriction, a listener mostly hears evening and night ragas as concerts are typically held at those times. However, while listening to the radio broadcast during different times of the day and at some music festivals, one does get to hear early morning, afternoon and late-night ragas.

NOMENCLATURE OF NOTES (SWARAS)

Though both systems use an octave consisting of twelve notes, the names used are different:

Carnatic Name	*Pronounced as*	*Hindustani Name*	*Pronounced as*
Shadjam	Sa	Shadaj	Sa
Shuddha Rishabham	Ri	Komal Rishab	Re
Chatusruti Rishabham	Ri	Shuddh Rishab	Re
Sadharana Gandharam	Ga	Komal Gandhar	Ga
Antara Gandharam	Ga	Shuddh Gandhar	Ga
Shuddha Madhyamam	Ma	Shuddh Madhyam	Ma
Prati Madhyamam	Ma	Tivra Madhyam	Ma
Panchamam	Pa	Pancham	Pa
Shuddha Dhaivatam	Da	Komal Dhaivat	Dha
Chatusruti Dhaivatam	Da	Shuddh Dhaivat	Dha
Kaisiki Nishadam	Ni	Komal Nishad	Ni
Kakali Nishadam	Ni	Shuddh Nishad	Ni

SYSTEM OF LEARNING

Learning methods in Carnatic music are highly systematised. Purandara Dasa, the father of Carnatic music, formulated beginners' scales (Swaravalis) and songs (Gitams). In the South, every guru invariably starts with the Swaravali, Jantai-varisai, sapta-tala alankaras, and so on before moving to full-length compositions. The raga taught in these beginners' scales is always Mayamalavagaula. This is a very logical choice as this scale has all the possible intervals in it: i.e. ½ note (one semi-tone) between Sa and Ri, Ga and Ma, Pa and Dha, Ni and Sa (octave higher); 1½ (three semi-tones) between Ri and Ga, Dha and Ni, and one whole note (two semi-tones) between Ma and Pa.

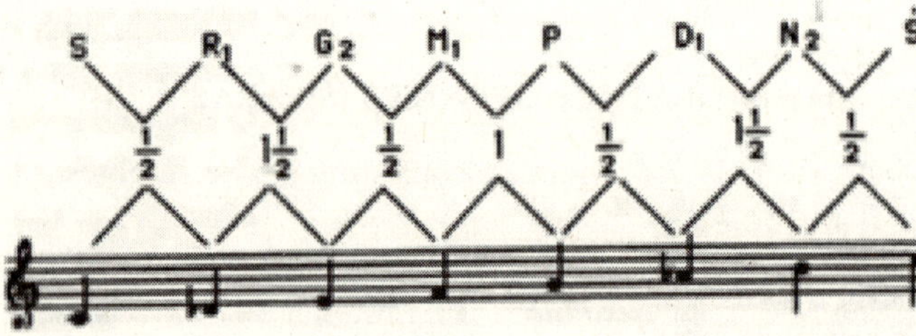

In the Hindustani system, there is no standardised system of learning. Depending on the guru, one starts with Raga Yaman or Bhairav or Bilawal.

RAGA DEVELOPMENT

In the Hindustani system, the raga is developed stage by stage, starting with a very slow tempo in the low register or lower octave with long sustaining notes. In the South, they do not always start in the lower register but rather with a phrase built around the vadi or samvadi, which conveys the essence of the raga. The tempo is also medium and all the notes are highly ornamented in contrast to the Hindustani system.

GHARANAS AND BANIS

In Western classical music, we talk about musical periods like Baroque, Classical, Romantic, Modern, etc. We can compare this in some sense to the system of gharanas in north Indian classical music and banis in south Indian classical music. When a great composer or creative genius enters the scene, they create a unique style of music that is adopted or imitated by others of that era. When many people begin to follow that particular style, it becomes crystallised. There are several gharanas like Agra, Bhendibazaar, Gwalior, Delhi, Indore, Jaipur-Atrauli, Kirana, Mewati, Patiala and Rampur-Sahaswan. Among *bani*s, we have those of great musicians like Alathur Brothers, Chembai Vaidyanatha Bhagavathar, D K Pattammal, G N Balasubramaniam, M S Subbulakshmi, Palghat Mani Iyer, Semmangudi Srinivasa Iyer, T N Rajarathinam Pillai, T R Mahalingam and many more.

SWARA-KALPANA

The art of swara-kalpana (improvisation based on sol-fa syllables) is highly developed in the south and the vocalists sing very complicated rhythmic patterns and calculations. Certain rhythmic figures are repeated three times to come back to the down-beat. These calculated patterns are done within the strict framework of the rules and sometimes in different nadais (refer to the chapter called Rhythmic Concept). The south also has the concept of the koraipu which does not exist in the north. This is where the vocalist sings along a phrase, which is followed by a similar phrase by the melodic accompanist (like the violinist), and this goes on, back and forth, with the length of these phrases getting gradually shorter and shorter, culminating in a calculated rhythmic pattern repeated three times to come back to the eduppu or the beginning of the composition. Some Hindustani instrumentalists (melodic and percussion) have adopted a few of these concepts effectively.

COMPOSITIONS

In the south, more compositional forms are used in-concert than in the north, because of the great wealth of compositions attributed to the trinity of composers – Tyagaraja, Muthuswamy Dikshitar and Shyama Shastri.

There are fewer traditional classical compositions in the north and they are short, usually no longer than two rhythmic cycles in length (except in some cases where the compositions are set to short talas like Jhaptal or Rupaktal – in which case it is more than two cycles). In the south, however, forms like Varnam, Swarajati, Kriti and Padam are much longer (refer to the chapter called Musical Forms).

INSTRUMENTS

The melodic instruments used in the south are the nagaswaram, veena, gotuvadyam, jaltarangam, etc., and percussion instruments are mridangam, tavil, khanjira, ghatam and morsing. In the north, the most commonly used melodic instruments are the sitar, surbahar, sarod, sarangi, shehnai and santoor; percussion instruments are the tabla, nagara and, occasionally, the pakhawaj. The flute, violin and the tambura (tanpura in the north) are common to both systems.

The violin has been adapted and used in the Carnatic tradition for a longer time than in the Hindustani system. After being introduced to Carnatic music by Baluswami Dikshitar, it became the most important accompanying instrument in concerts. In due course, it has also emerged as a major solo instrument. In the north, solo performances are the rule, since the sarangi and the harmonium are more frequently used than the violin for accompanying vocal music. There are also fewer violinists in the north as compared to the south.

VOCAL AND INSTRUMENTAL FORMS

In the south, all the musical forms are vocal, with texts, which are also played on the various instruments. In the north, there are compositions exclusive to vocal (khyal, thumri, tarana, etc.) and to instruments (gat, dhun, etc).

MELODIC ACCOMPANIMENT

There are some major differences between Hindustani and Carnatic music on the basis of the role of the melodic accompaniment. In the case of vocal music, both systems use melodic accompaniment, be it a violin or a sarangi or harmonium. In the case of an instrumental concert in the north, the only accompaniment is the percussion. Whereas, in the south, instrumental concerts like veena, flute, etc, are invariably accompanied by the violin and percussion(s). The most common melodic accompanying instruments in the north are the harmonium and the sarangi, whereas the most common accompaniment in the south is the violin. In the north, the accompanist generally provides support and provides some fillers when the soloist lets him. But, in the south, the role of the accompanist is extremely demanding. He is expected to play on par with the soloist, play all the compositions along with him, play a solo raga improvisation after the soloist and improvise based on the sol-fa syllables (swara-kalpana), and take an almost equal turn each time the soloist does so. The accompanist has a lot of scope to reveal his talent.

PERCUSSION ACCOMPANIMENT

There are some major differences between the north Indian and south Indian musical systems when it comes to the role of the percussion instruments. In the north, the tabla player usually provides support to the vocal or melodic instrument and plays the 'theka' (fixed patterns for each rhythmic cycle) – which provides the soloist with a frame of reference. The concept of the theka does not exist in the south. The mridangam and the secondary percussion usually improvise along with the soloist and try to follow the rhythmic patterns that the soloist is playing. This is why, in the south, the vocalists normally indicate the tala using hand gestures and instrumentalists sometimes have people who act as tala-keepers. In a percussion ensemble, the percussionists take turns and keep the tala while the others play. In the north, this is not necessary as the theka constantly indicates one's position in the cycle.

Additionally, in the south, the tani avartanam is a traditional part of the concert. Here, the percussion(s) are given a solo to display their virtuosity and skill. In the north, the vocalists or instrumentalists allow the percussionist short solos as fillers between their own improvisational sections while they often repeat the first line of the composition. In recent years, some of the main artists of the north have started allowing percussionists to play longer solos like in the south.

SECONDARY PERCUSSIONS

The concept of secondary percussion instruments does not exist in the north. There is only a single percussion instrument like the tabla and the pakhawaj, whereas in the south there are various secondary percussion instruments (or upa-pakkavadyam as they are called) like the khanjira, ghatam and morsing.

TEMPO CHANGES

In the north, one starts the concert at a slow speed and gradually builds up tempo during the course of the improvisation. In the south, however, this is not allowed. The basic tempo almost always remains the same, but the musician gets faster and faster during improvisation by playing more number of notes, systematically using different nadais and kalas.

COMPLEXITIES OF COMPOSITION

In Carnatic forms like the varnam and the ragam-tanam-pallavi, performers often render the compositions in multiple speeds (see tri-kalam under ragam-tanam-pallavi). There are also compositions in pancha-nadais involving all the five nadais. This is a feature unique to the Carnatic tradition.

MUSICAL FORMS

In the south Indian system, there are specific forms which are used for opening the concert—like the varnam or a kriti. The varnam, if performed, is always the opening piece and it is never sung or played in the latter part of the concert. The ragam-tanam-pallavi is always performed during the latter part of the concert. Similarly, the tillana and javali are performed towards the end of the concert as light forms. The mangalam is always the final piece. north India has fewer musical forms than the South.

The musical forms of the two systems are very different from each other. The ragam-tanam portion of the ragam-tanam-pallavi form is the only thing that resembles the alap, jod, jhala section of Hindustani music. The dhrupad style of alap and jod is very similar to the Carnatic ragam-tanam section.

COMPOSITION VS. IMPROVISATION

In a Hindustani concert, one hears more improvisation and less composed numbers as performed in the Carnatic system. A typical Hindustani concert has two to three major pieces with elaborate improvisations based on very short compositions. A typical Carnatic vocal concert has eight or more compositions, some of them including kritis sung without any improvisation.

TALA SYSTEM

The south has a system of one hundred and seventy-five talas, in addition to which there is the group of chapu-talas. In the north, fewer talas are in common use. Also, as explained earlier, the whole rhythmic concept in the south is extremely complex, but, at the same time, very methodically worked out.

CONCERT FORMAT

A Hindustani concert begins with an elaborate raga improvisation. There is no set format for a concert in the north; it varies from one performer to the other. One musician may sing only khyals and tarana, another may sing khyal and thumri, and yet another may choose akhyal, thumri and bhajan.

In a Carnatic concert, however, the musician starts either with a varnam or a kriti in praise of the deity Ganesha. This is typically followed by a few kritis and an elaborate alapana around the middle of the concert, either before a major kriti or in a ragam-tanam-pallavi. After this, lighter pieces like padams, javalis or tillanas are sung. The traditional end is the mangalam.

SPIRITUAL BASE

Carnatic music has a very strong spiritual base. Almost all the compositions by the trinity and other leading composers are based on Hindu religion, philosophy and mythology as opposed to Hindustani music, where the compositions range from romantic and erotic to spiritual. However, in Carnatic music, forms like the padam and javali often have romantic themes.

As mentioned in the chapter on Melodic Concept, in recent times, there has been an exchange of ragas between the two systems in some Carnatic concerts; it is not uncommon to hear a bhajan or two that have been adapted from the Hindustani system. However, a north Indian musician hardly ever plays a Carnatic musical form in his/her concert.

It is interesting to note that several south Indian musicians have been extremely successful performers of Hindustani music but the reverse is yet to happen. Also, one sees many more south Indians at a Hindustani concert than one sees north Indians at a Carnatic concert, though that is slowly changing.

7

Musical Instruments

The ancient Indian classification in Bharata's *Natyashastra* puts musical instruments into four categories:

1. Tata vadya (stringed instruments)
2. Susira vadya (hollow instruments)
3. Avanaddha vadya (covered instruments)
4. Ghana vadya (solid instruments)

This is very similar to the classification of instruments published in 1914 by Erich von Hornbostel and Curt Sachs, as follows:

1. Chordophones
2. Aerophones
3. Membranophones
4. Idiophones

If we overlay Bharata's and the von Hornbostel/Sachs classification, we find that tata vadyas correspond to chordophones, susira vadyas to aerophones, avanaddha vadyas to membranophones, and ghana vadyas to idiophones.

Tata vadyas (chordophones or stringed instruments) produce sound through the vibrations of a stretched string.

Susira vadyas (aerophones or wind instruments) produce sound through the vibration of a column of air. The shape of the instrument is such that the vibrations are of a particular length, determining the particular pitch.

Avanaddha vadyas (membranophones) are a type of percussion instrument. They produce sound through the vibrations of a membrane or skin, which is usually stretched across a resonator.

Ghana vadyas (idiophones) are also percussion instruments, but in these sound is produced by the vibrations of the instruments themselves when they are struck or hit. Idiophones are classified by what action causes them to vibrate and produce sound.

TABLE 7.1
Musical Instruments

Tata vadya	*Susira vadya*	*Avanaddha vadya*	*Ghana vadya*
a) **Plucked**			
Tambura	Flute	Mridangam	Jalatarangam
Veena	Nagaswaram	Tavil	Ghatam
Gotuvadyam	Ottu	Kanjira	Morsing
Guitar	Harmonium	Tabla	Jalra
Mandolin	Shehnai	Tabla Tarang	
Sitar	Saxophone	Pakhawaj	
Surbahar		Nagara	
Sarod			
Vichitra Veena			
Swaramandal			
b) **Bowed**			
Violin			
Viola			
Esraj			
Dilruba			
Tar-shehnai			
c) **Struck**			
Santoor			

The list of instruments used in Indian classical music is a dynamic one. New instruments are being adopted or adapted into traditional forms of music on a regular basis. Some instruments have been a part of Indian classical music for centuries, like the veena, while others are fairly new, like the saxophone or mandolin.

CHORDOPHONES OR STRINGED INSTRUMENTS

Tambura

The tambura, a classical drone instrument, is a very important part of every Indian concert. This instrument is common to both the north and south Indian systems, though the names and the construction vary slightly. In the north, it is called the tanpura. The tambura player usually sits behind the main artist and plays the instrument throughout the concert, starting just before the main artist starts and ending after the main artist stops, providing a constant drone.

The tambura has between four and six strings. In the four-stringed tambura, the first string is tuned to the dominant, the middle strings are tuned to the tonic, and the last, which is the bass string, to the tonic, an octave lower. In the five- and six-stringed tamburas, the extra strings can be tuned to either tonic and dominant or other notes in the raga.

Made of wood (usually jackwood), the tambura has a long unfretted neck. The neck has a bowl-shaped resonator at the lower end, which vibrates and amplifies the sound. In the south Indian tambura this resonator is made of wood, whereas in the north Indian tanpura it is usually made out of a hollow, seasoned gourd.

At the upper end of the long neck are tuning pegs, below which is a thin plate placed perpendicular to the neck. This plate has holes through which the strings pass. The strings next pass over a narrow, grooved plate, below the first perpendicular plate, run along the entire length of the neck, and over a broad, grooved bridge, usually made of bone or ivory, which sits on the resonator. The strings are then attached to the bottom of the bowl. Between the attachment

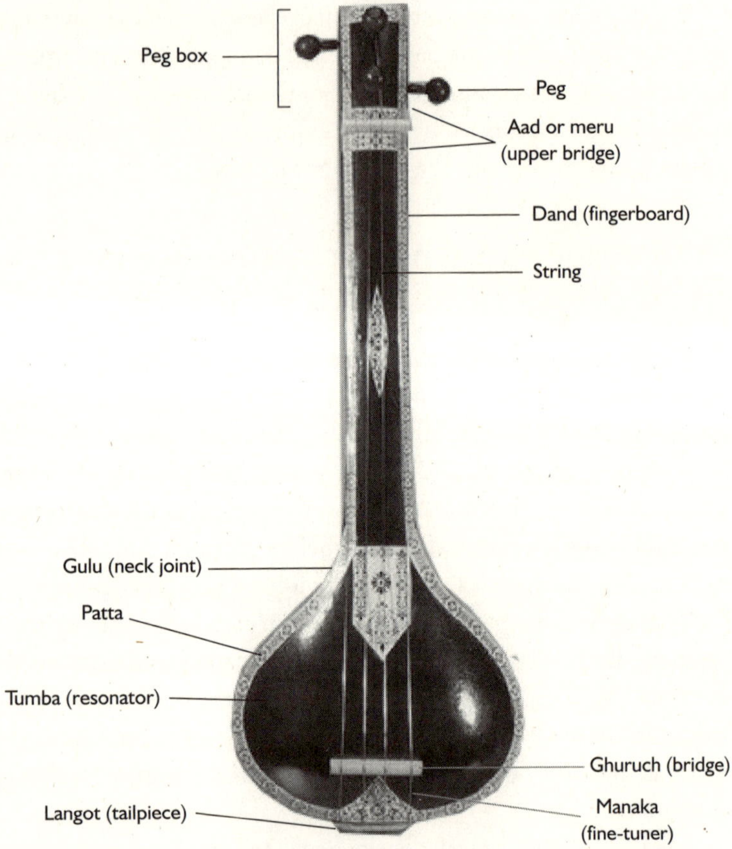

and the bridge, a bead is strung through each string and serves as a fine-tuner when moved up or down. Also, fine silk threads, known as jiva, are used between the bridge and the strings. When positioned perfectly, these threads cause the strings to 'buzz' and enhance the tonal quality. This is a characteristic feature of the tambura.

Playing position: The tambura is normally held vertically on the right side of the lap of the performer. The strings are plucked in succession, starting with the first string and ending with the bass string, with the middle and forefingers of the right hand, while the resonator is usually supported by the left hand.

In some cases, like with north Indian tanpuras with large gourds, the tanpura is placed vertically on the floor before the player and the right leg, bent at the knee, is used to support the gourd.

It is also occasionally placed horizontally across the performer's lap.

Veena

The veena is one of the most important instruments of south India. The modern veena has evolved from its ancient counterpart after undergoing several modifications. In ancient times, the veena had several strings tuned to different notes. The instrument was played on open strings. Later, the number of strings was reduced and there were movable frets. This gave way to the modern veena with twenty-four fixed frets, which covers three-and-a-half octaves. Govinda Dikshitar, who was the prime minister of Raghunatha Nayak, the seventeenth-century ruler of Thanjavur, perfected this veena. In other words, the modern veena is only three centuries old.

In ancient literature, the word 'veena' was used to describe both the lute and harp type of instruments. In the latter type, a number of strings were stretched over an open frame. The strings were plucked with the fingers and each string produced only one note. The strings were tuned to notes of absolute pitch and to the fundamental scale. A veena with a fingerboard but without frets can be seen in the Ajanta paintings. This type of veena was held at an angle when played, whereas the harp type was held vertically. The addition of frets to the veena was a very important step in its evolution. The number of strings were reduced. This facilitated the playing of gamakas by pulling on the strings.

In the modern veena the strings are tuned to a relative pitch. Any one note is taken as the tonic, or adhara shadja, and the other strings are tuned in relation to that note.

Made of jackwood, the veena consists of a hollow resonator carved out of a single block of wood that continues as a long, fretted neck, to which is attached another smaller resonator. The neck curves

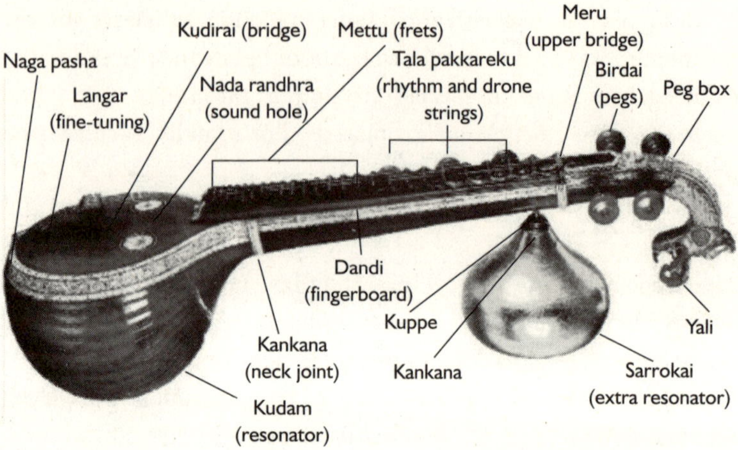

backwards and at the end is a carved head of a mythological animal. On the flat portion of the resonator sits a brass-plated bridge and through its grooves run the four main strings. At the end of the main resonator is a string holder. Below the bridge, which sits on the resonator, are small metal rings attached on one side to the strings and on the other to the string holder by thick metal wires. Between the rings and the string holder are small metal coils for finer tuning. Attached to the right side of the main bridge is a curved metal bridge over which pass the three tala strings. These strings are used for keeping the drone and also to indicate the rhythmic cycle. The three strings are attached to pegs on the side of the neck. The four main strings run along the length of the neck, pass over a grooved plate into four tuning pegs, two on either side of the neck. The neck is carved out and covered with a thin strip of wood. On both sides of the neck are wax ledges with twenty-four frets between them. The smaller resonator, which is attached to the underside of the neck, is made either of papier mâché or a carved-out gourd. This serves as a second or additional resonator and also as a rest. This gourd is detachable.

Playing position: It may be held either vertically or horizontally, the latter position being more commonly used. The performer sits cross-legged and holds the veena with the small resonator resting on the left thigh. The index and middle fingers of the left hand are used to press down on the strings against the frets, while the index and middle fingers of the right hand are used to pluck the strings at the lower end. The player normally wears a wire plectrum on both fingers. Ornamentations (gamakas) are produced by pulling the strings. The little finger is used to pluck the tala strings. Tala strings are plucked upwards while the main strings are plucked downwards.

Gotuvadyam

The gotuvadyam is also known as the mahanataka veena or the banumad veena. It is structured like the veena, but without frets and the wax ledge. In addition, there are sympathetic strings, which form the lower layer. Usually made of jackwood, the gotuvadyam has twenty-one strings which are divided thus: the six strings on the upper layer are the main playing strings, three strings on the side are the tala or rhythm/drone strings and twelve sympathetic strings run beneath the main strings. The main strings are tuned to tonics and dominants. Of the twelve sympathetic strings, four are tuned to Sa,

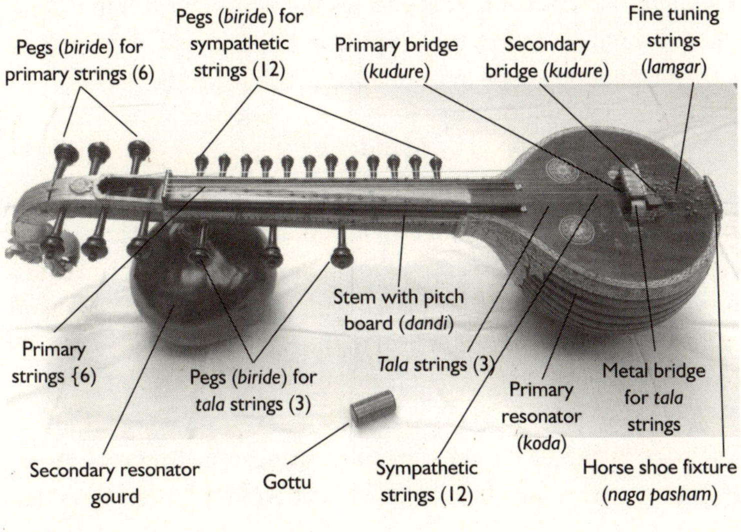

three are tuned to Pa, and the other five to Ri, Ga, Ma, Dha and Ni (depending on the raga).

Playing position: The instrument is placed horizontally in front of the seated performer. A wooden or metal cylinder, four to six inches long and about an inch in diametre , held in the left hand is used to slide over the strings, which are simultaneously plucked with the middle and forefinger of the right hand. The little finger is used to pluck the tala strings. As in the case of the veena, the main strings are plucked downwards and the tala strings upwards.

Guitar

The guitar used in Indian music is adapted from the Western guitar. It is a plucked string instrument. The modern guitar has six strings tuned to E, A, D, G, B, E, and has a three-octave range. The instrument has a waisted body shape, and a flat back and soundboard. It has a fretted neck over which the strings pass.

Playing position: It is placed on the lap of the performer, and played like the Hawaiian slide guitar, with a plectrum in the right hand and a slide in the left hand. This enables the performer to produce all the slides and ornamentations typical to Indian music. It can also be played without the slide in the left hand, using just the fingers.

Mandolin

The mandolin used in Indian music is the Western mandolin, a small instrument that resembles a lute. It evolved in Italy around the eighteenth century. It usually has four pairs of strings that run over a fretted neck. The strings are played with the fingers of the left hand and plucked with a plectrum held in the right hand.

Sitar

The sitar is one of the most popular stringed instruments in the Hindustani tradition. It is believed that Amir Khusrau modified the veena to create the sitar. His version had three strings and was known as seh-tar (seh meaning three in his mother tongue Persian, and tar meaning strings).

It is made of teak wood and seasoned gourds. It has a long neck with twenty movable metal frets and five to seven main strings. Two of these strings are known as the chikari, which are used as drone strings and also to create a rhythmic effect during the fast improvisational sections (known as jhala). Below the frets run sympathetic strings, varying between nine and thirteen in number, which are tuned to the notes of the raga being played. At the lower end of the neck is a gourd, which acts as the resonator. On the gourd sits a large bridge over which run the main strings and below these strings, close to the main bridge, sits another smaller bridge, over which run the sympathetic strings. The bridges are normally made of ivory or bone. There may be another gourd, as in the veena (which is a more recent addition), at the upper end, which acts as a secondary resonator. The frets are convex and are tied to the neck. The frets can be moved up or down to get a particular pitch to suit the notes of the raga being played.

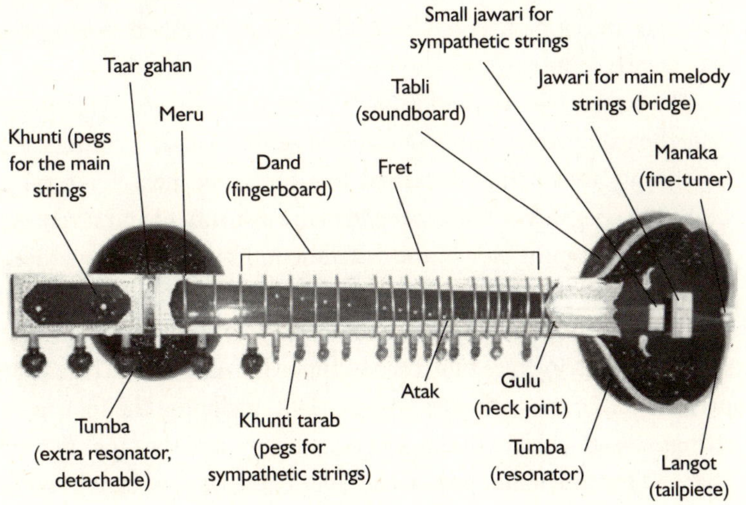

Playing position: The sitar is held at about an angle of forty-five degrees to the floor. The main resonator rests on the left foot of the cross-legged seated performer. The right elbow of the seated performer rests on and supports the resonator. The main strings are played with the fingers of the left hand and, at the same time, plucked by a wire plectrum (known as mijrah) worn on the index finger of the right hand. The little finger is used to strum the sympathetic strings and, at times, the chikari strings. A very typical feature of this instrument is the 'pulling' of the strings sideways with the fingers of the left hand, to slide from one note to another, sometimes covering almost an octave. This type of ornamentation is known as meend.

Surbahar

This is a larger version of the sitar, with a deeper bass tone. The main gourd is a little flatter and the strings are thicker than those of the sitar. Due to its bass quality and thicker strings, this instrument is used more for the alap.

Sarod

It is believed that the sarod originally came from Afghanistan and was developed from the Middle Eastern rabab during the nineteenth century.

The sarod has a wooden body covered with goatskin and a fingerboard covered with a polished sheet of steel. It is fretless and has twenty-five strings, attached to twenty-five pegs for tuning. Eight large pegs are at the upper end of the instrument and seventeen smaller pegs on the side of the instrument. Fifteen are sympathetic strings. These pass through tiny holes in the metal fingerboard and are attached to small tuning pegs on the side of the instrument. The sympathetic strings are tuned according to the notes in the raga to be performed. Of the other ten strings, eight, including the four main strings, are attached to the large pegs at the top, and the other two are attached to the smaller pegs at the side. These last two strings serve to accentuate the percussive rhythm. The first four are tuned to the

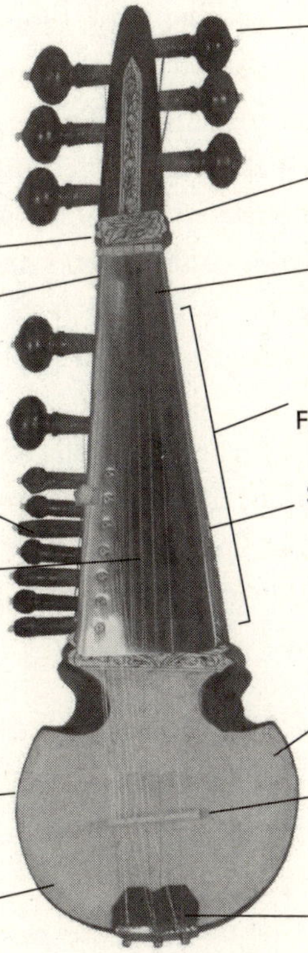

dominant notes of the raga to be played and serve as drone strings. A metal gourd attached to the top end acts as a resonator. This was a later addition.

Playing position: The sarod is held on the lap of the cross-legged performer. The fingers of the left hand are used to press the strings down and slide along the fingerboard, while the strings are plucked with a triangular plectrum, made of a coconut shell, held in the right hand.

Vichitra Veena

The vichitra veena is very similar to the gotuvadyam. It consists of an unfretted, long neck, which is attached to a gourd at each end. The gourds act as resonators. There are six main strings, which pass over a bridge, run along the length of the neck and then attach to pegs on the side at one end of the instrument. Besides the main strings, there are two chikari strings that are used intermittently when playing the jhala. These are like the tala strings of the gotuvadyam. Under the bridge and the main strings run eleven sympathetic strings, which are attached to pegs on the side of the neck (facing the performer) and are tuned to the note of the raga to be played.

Playing position: The instrument is placed horizontally, with the gourds resting on the floor in front of the seated player. The player slides a glass ball held in the left hand over the strings and, at the same time, plucks the strings with a wire plectrum worn on the fingers of the right hand.

Violin

The violin is believed to have been introduced to Indian music by Baluswami Dikshitar in the early nineteenth century.

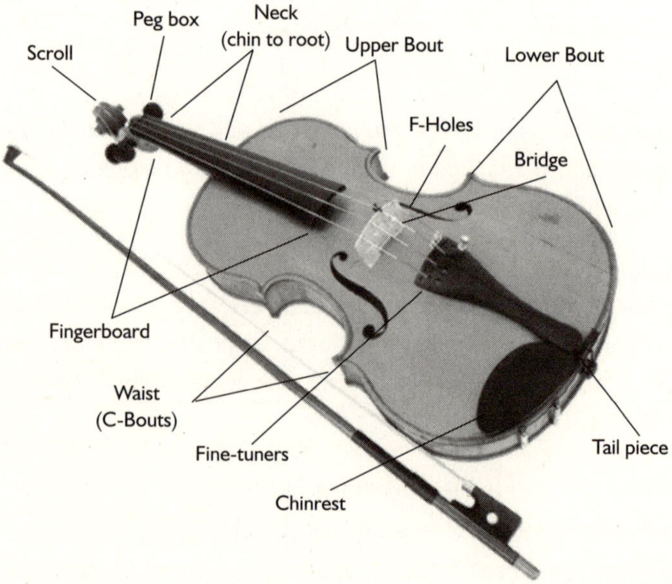

The south Indian violin is almost identical to the Western violin in structure, but differs from it in tuning and playing position. It is traditionally played sitting cross-legged, with the scroll placed on the artist's right ankle and the back of the violin resting on the left shoulder (collarbone or chest), thus giving the performer an unencumbered left hand with which to play Indian musical ornamentations such as the gamaka. It is tuned as follows: tonic, dominant, tonic (octave higher) and dominant (octave higher), from the fourth to the first string respectively, the tonic being variable.

In addition to being a main instrument in concerts, the Carnatic violin is a necessary melodic accompaniment in both vocal and instrumental concerts (except for the nagaswaram).

In Hindustani music, the violin is primarily a solo and secondarily an accompanying instrument. Although the position of holding the violin and the tuning are similar in both Carnatic and Hindustani music, the style of playing and the ornamentations are different.

Sarangi

The sarangi is one of the oldest bowed instruments. Myth has it that it was invented by Ravana (the king of Lanka in the Ramayana) and is, therefore, also known as the Ravanahasta. Initially, it was a rudimentary, probably folk, fiddle and it is believed that it got its present form from Amir Khusrau.

The body is hollow and made of teak wood, inlaid with ivory decorations. The soundbox is covered with goatskin and the fretless fingerboard with wood. Three of its thirty-eight strings are the main strings while the rest are sympathetic strings. The three main strings are usually gut strings attached at the top of the instrument to three large pegs, and run over an ivory bridge that sits on the skin. Of the thirty-five sympathetic strings, eleven are attached to small pegs on the topmost part of the instrument in front, and the other twenty-four are attached to pegs at the side.

The sarangi has been mainly an accompaniment for vocal music but has now become a solo instrument.

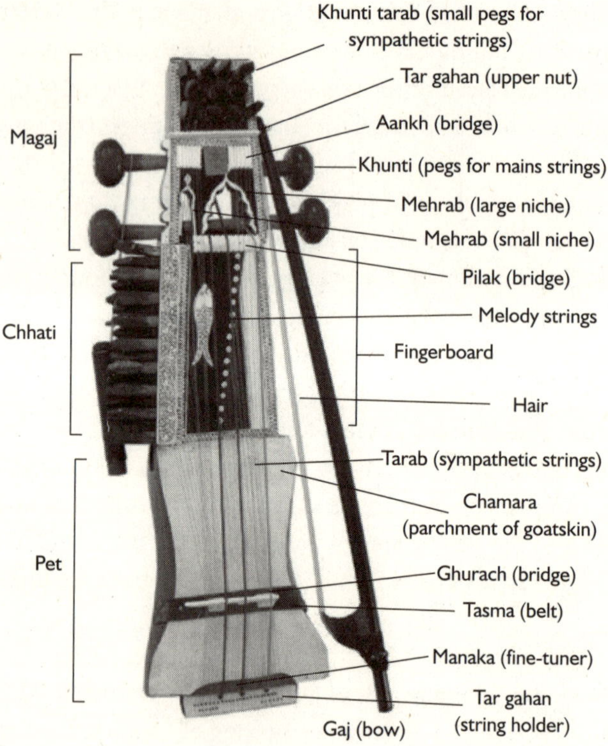

Playing position: The sarangi is held in a vertical position with the tip resting on the performer's left shoulder, and played with a heavy convex bow. The bow is held in the right hand with the palm facing upwards, the thumb pressing the tip of the bow and the index and second fingers touching the wooden stick, while the third and little fingers are slipped between the stick and resin-coated horsehair. The instrument is played by pressing the cuticles of the left hand against the strings.

Esraj

The esraj is a cross between the sitar and the sarangi in construction. The top half resembles the sitar and the lower half is like the sarangi. In other words, the top half has a long, fretted neck and the lower

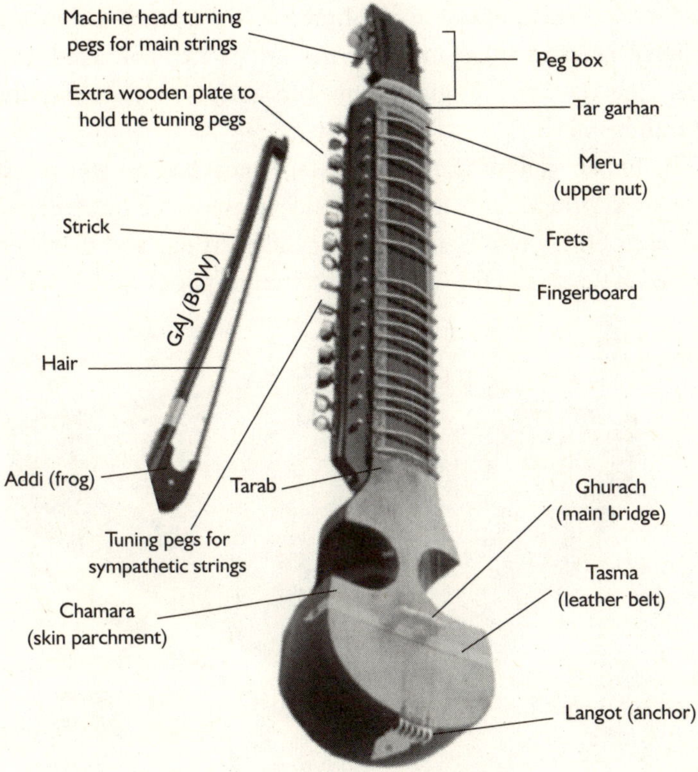

half consists of a sound box covered with skin on which sits the bridge, over which run the strings that are played with a bow. The esraj has four strings and sixteen frets on the neck.

Playing position: It rests on the lap of the seated player and is supported against his left shoulder. The first and second fingers of the left hand are used to press the strings down against the frets whilst bowing the strings with the right hand.

Santoor

Also known as shata-tantri veena (hundred-stringed veena), the santoor was originally a folk instrument that came to India from

Persia and is still popular in Kashmir. It is a type of hammered dulcimer or board zither in which the strings are hammered with sticks (the dulcimer originated in Persia and Iraq around the eleventh century).

The Indian santoor is a wooden trapezoidal box on which rest thirty small bridges, fifteen on each side, close to the outer edges. Over each bridge passes a set of four metal strings and these are attached at the side of the instrument to tuning pegs.

Playing position: The santoor is placed on the lap of the performer and the strings are struck with two light wooden tongs, one in each hand. The tongs are slightly curved at the ends that strike the strings, and at the other ends are shaped like hooks where the index finger is inserted and held with the thumb pressed on top of the hook. This helps the performer get a light but firm grip of the tongs.

AEROPHONES OR WIND INSTRUMENTS

Flute

The flute is one of the oldest wind instruments. It is known as murali or venu in Sanskrit and kuzhal in Tamil. It is one of the three instruments mentioned in ancient Indian literature, the other two being the veena and the mridangam. Originally a folk instrument, it is associated with Lord Krishna.

The bamboo flute, which is the most commonly used flute in Indian classical music, is a natural instrument without detachable parts or a complicated mechanism. Flutes can also be made of sandalwood, ebony, iron, bell metal or precious metals like silver and gold.

The flute is usually a simple cylindrical tube with uniformly drilled holes, closed at one end. Flutes vary in length from eight inches to two-and-a-half feet. The longer flutes have a deeper bass tone whereas the shorter ones are higher pitched.

The south Indian flute is usually about fourteen inches in length and three-quarters of an inch in diametre . The closed end may be naturally closed by the node of the bamboo stem, or artificially sealed with a cork or a stopper. About three quarters of an inch from the sealed end is the mouth hole known as the mukha randara. Besides the mouth hole, there are eight finger holes of uniform size in a straight line. The finger holes are slightly smaller than the mouth hole. The finger hole closest to the mouth hole is called the tara randara, that is, the hole which produces the highest pitch of all the holes. This is considered to be the first hole and the rest are numbered in progression.

The Hindustani flute is known as the bansuri (which comes from the Hindi word 'bans' for bamboo).

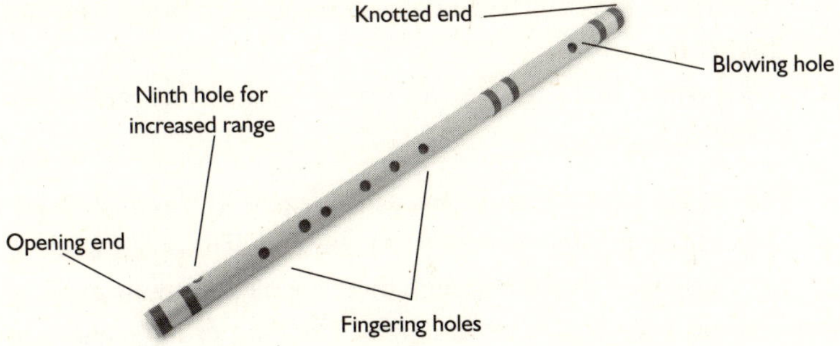

The flute is a delicate instrument and one that can produce all the ornamentations, curves, slides and nuances that are characteristic of Indian music. The flute has a range of two-and-a-half octaves. It was used as an accompanying instrument for music and dance.

Playing position: The flute is held horizontally, normally to the player's right, slightly inclined downwards. It rests on the two thumbs. The first three fingers of the left hand and the four fingers of the right hand are used to close finger holes one to seven respectively. The eighth finger hole is left open. Sound is produced by blowing air at an angle against the opposite edge of the mouth hole. The lower lip covers a part of the mouth hole. Variations in pitch are caused by altering the effective length of the air column as a result of opening and closing the air holes. Semitones and quartertones can be produced by the partial opening and closing of the finger holes.

Nagaswaram

The nagaswaram is known as a mangala vadya (or auspicious instrument), since it is played in temples, processions, festivals and on auspicious occasions like marriages. The correct name, incidentally, is nagaswaram and not nadaswaram as pronounced by some. Not more than about eight hundred years old, it is also known as nayanam in Tamil.

There are two varieties of nagaswarams:

1. Timiri, which is shorter (usually about one-and-a-half feet) and higher in pitch
2. Pari, which is longer (two to two-and-a-half feet) and lower in pitch.

The nagaswaram is a double-reed instrument with a conical bore, which gradually enlarges towards the lower end. It is usually made of a type of seasoned ebony, although there are nagaswarams made of sandalwood, redwood, silver and gold. The top portion consists of

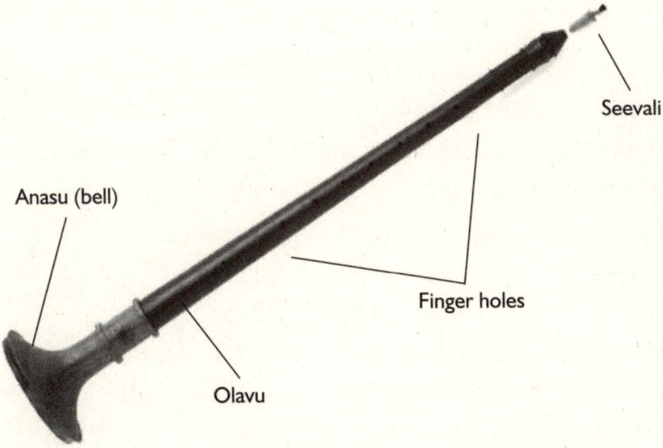

a metal staple (called mel anaichu) and into this is inserted a small metallic cylinder called kendai. The kendai carries the mouthpiece, known as narukku or sivali, which is made of reed. Along with spare reeds, a small needle, known as 'kuchchi' and made of ivory or horn, is attached to the nagaswaram. The needle is used to clear the mouth hole of saliva particles and allow air to pass through. The bottom is decorated with a metallic bell called the keezh anaichu.

The nagaswaram has seven finger holes. There are five additional holes drilled at the bottom, which are used as controllers. Like the flute, the nagaswaram has a range of two-and-a-half octaves. The system of fingering is like that used in the flute. But whereas in the flute, seminotes and quarternotes are produced by the partial opening and closing of the finger holes, in the nagaswaram they are produced by adjusting the column of air blown into the pipe. This makes it a very strenuous instrument to play.

It is a very loud instrument, which makes it more suitable for open-air and outdoor performances than indoor concerts.

The nagaswaram ensemble is known as the periya melam and generally consists of a lead nagaswaram player, the ottu or drone, tavil player and a tala keeper with a pair of bronze cymbals (jalra).

Ottu

The ottu is a drone instrument that is part of the nagaswaram ensemble. It is similar to the nagaswaram in shape and structure but is slightly longer. The player holds the reed at the upper end of the instrument in his mouth and blows into it to provide a single note, which serves as a drone for the nagaswaram.

Harmonium

The harmonium came to India from the West and has been very popular for accompanying light music. The harmonium is a kind of portable organ. It is a reed organ with a keyboard that spans over two-and-a-half octaves. It has a set of reeds but, unlike the organ, has no pipes. It works on a system of bellows, which make the reeds vibrate when the keys are pressed down. This is more commonly used in north Indian classical music as an accompaniment for vocal concerts. In the south, it is used more in concerts of light music and bhajan groups (groups that sing devotional songs). The keys are tuned to a tempered scale, like the piano, which limits it when it comes to ornamentations in Indian classical music.

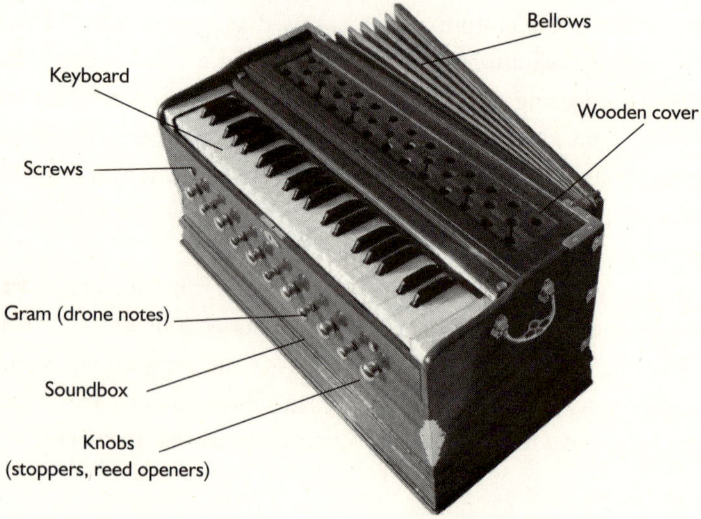

Playing position: The player sits on the floor with the instrument in front of him and operates the bellows with the left hand, while playing on the keyboard with the fingers of the right hand.

Shehnai

It is believed that the shehnai came to India from Persia. It is an oboe-like instrument, which is very loud and associated with auspicious occasions like marriages and temple processions in Hindustani music, like the nagaswaram in Carnatic music. This was originally a folk instrument but has now become a solo classical instrument.

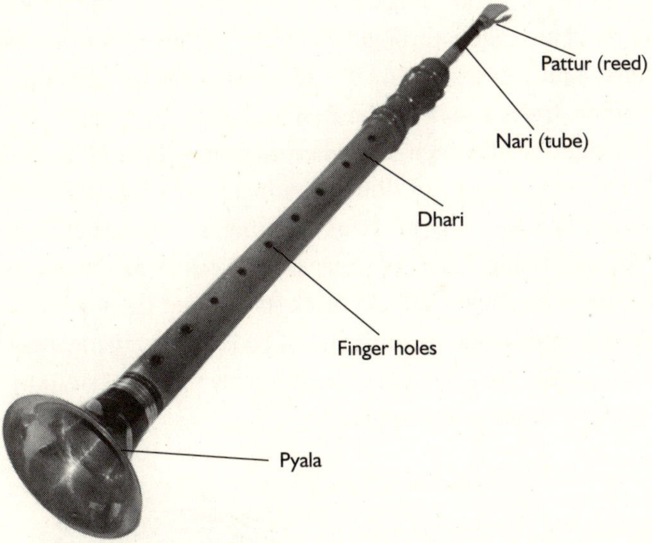

It is a double-reed instrument made of hard wood, with a conical bore that gradually enlarges towards the lower end. A metallic bell usually decorates this end. It has finger holes on the body and different pitches are produced by varying the pressure by air blown through the reed and also by the opening and closing of the finger holes.

MEMBRANOPHONES OR PERCUSSION INSTRUMENTS

Mridangam

The mridangam, the classical drum of south India, is used as an accompaniment in vocal, instrumental and dance performances.

Mridangam literally means 'clay-body', which indicates that it was originally made of clay. The mridangam in use today is made of a single block of wood that has been hollowed out. The wood used is either jackwood or redwood, though sometimes the core of the coconut or palm tree is also used. It is a double-headed drum shaped like a barrel. The two heads are made of layers of skin stretched by leather straps that run along the sides of the body. On the rims of the heads there are spaces through which the leather straps pass. Small cylindrical pieces of wood are placed between the wooden shell and the leather straps, and can be moved to change the pitch.

The right head, which is smaller than the left head, is made of three concentric layers of skin. The innermost layer is not visible. The outer layer, usually made of calf hide, is called the meetu tol and the inner ring, made of sheepskin, is called the chapu tol. At the centre of the right head is a black spot, called the soru. This is a permanent spot made of a mixture of cooked rice, manganese and iron filings. This is what gives the mridangam its special tone. The right head is tuned to the tonic.

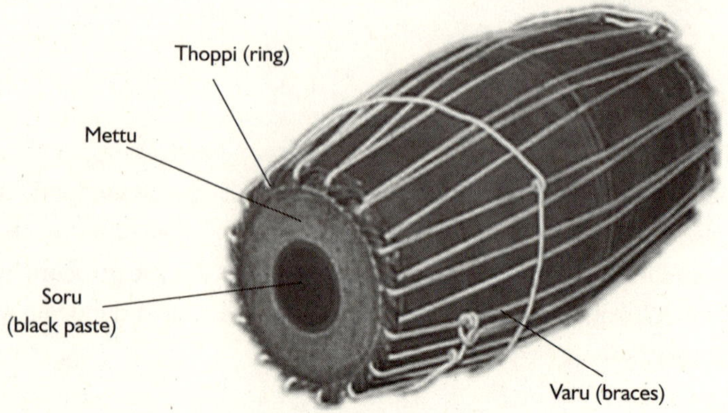

The left head, known as the toppi, is made of only two layers of skin. The inner layer is made of sheepskin and the outer layer is made of buffalo hide. Before playing, the performer applies a thick paste of semolina or cream of wheat to the centre of the left head. This is done to lower the pitch and give the mridangam a bass sound. Both heads are tuned by hitting the outer rims with a small wooden stick and a small, smooth stone. Striking the rim from the inside with downward strokes raises the pitch and striking it from the underside with upward strikes lowers the pitch. The left head is tuned to the tonic, an octave lower.

The mridangam is played with both hands, palms and fingers. The pitch of the mridangam varies with its size. The larger the mridangam, the lower the pitch and the smaller the mridangam, the higher the pitch. The lower pitched mridangams are known as taggu shruti and usually range from C to E (or 1 to 3 as it is known in Tamil) and the higher pitched mridangams are known as hechchu shruti and are usually between F and G sharp (4 to 5½).

Tavil

The tavil is the drum that is traditionally used with the nagaswaram ensemble or the periya melam. A double-headed drum, it is made from a solid block of wood hollowed out to form a cylindrical shape. The wood is generally jackwood. The solid block is about sixteen inches long and about thirteen-and-a-half inches in diametre . The walls of the tavil are generally between an eighth to a tenth of an inch in thickness. The two heads are made of skin stretched over hoops of hemp and bamboo sticks bundled together, on either side of the cylinder. The hoops are fastened by interlaced leather straps or braces. A band of leather runs over the braces around the middle of the drum and is used to tune the instrument. The tightening of the band stretches the skin and raises the pitch.

The drum is placed on the lap of the seated performer. The left head is played with a thick stick and the right head is played with the fingers of the right hand. Caps made of hardened rice paste are worn

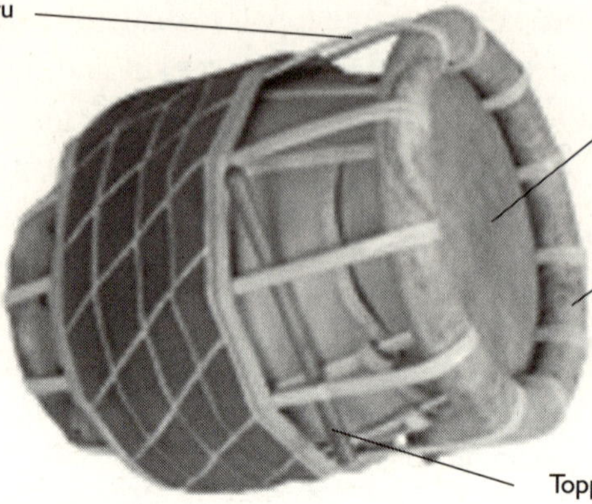

on the right fingers. Rings made of the same material are also worn on the knuckles of the right hand. The right head is stretched tight but is not tuned to any particular pitch.

When the tavil is played in a procession, with the nagaswaram, it is hung around the neck of the performer by a strap and played while the performer stands or walks.

The tavil is a very loud instrument. The tone is very different from that of the mridangam. Due to the stretched skin and the rice caps, the tone is very crisp and sharp.

As mentioned before, it was the traditional accompaniment to the nagaswaram but in recent years it has been used with other instruments like the violin.

Khanjira

A very old percussion instrument, the khanjira is a secondary percussion that is played with the mridangam. Similar to the Western tambourine, it consists of a circular wooden frame eight to nine inches in diametre and three to four inches in depth. The playing head is formed by a lizard skin stretched over one side of the frame. The other side is left open. The frame has three or four slits with small metal discs. These jingle when the khanjira is played. The khanjira is held in the left hand and played with the palm and

fingers of the right hand. The tension of the playing head can be reduced by sprinkling some water on it. Variations in sound can be produced by putting pressure near the outer rim, with the left hand, while playing. The instrument is not tuned to any particular pitch. Unlike the mridangam and the ghatam, the same khanjira can be used for any pitch.

Tabla

The tabla is the most common and popular accompanying percussion instrument used in Hindustani music today. Believed to have developed from the ancient pakhawaj in the thirteenth century, the word 'tabla' probably comes from the Arabic drum known as the tabl. It consists of a pair of drums: the right drum is known as the tabla (though both are collectively known as tabla) and the left drum is called the bayan (left in Hindi) or the dagga. The right drum is also sometimes called the dayan (right in Hindi). The tabla is made of wood and the head is made of stretched skin. The skin is stretched by leather straps that run down the side of the drum

over cylindrical blocks of wood used to tune the head. Finer tuning is done by striking the rim of the tabla with a small hammer. The tabla is the higher pitched drum which is usually tuned to the tonic (Sa), dominant (Pa) or the subdominant (Ma). The bayan is the bass drum and is usually made of metal with a stretched skin head. Both drums have a black spot in the centre made of manganese or iron dust (called syahi).

The instrument is placed in front of the performer who sits cross-legged. The bayan is played with the left hand, using the heel of the palm, the tips of the fingers and also the open palm placed on the head to produce a variety of sounds. The tabla is played with the right hand with the palm resting on the edge of the drum most of the time, and the fingers playing strokes on the different parts of the drum head.

Tabla Tarang

(Tarang means wave in Hindustani.) It consists of a group of tablas (only the right drums, not the bayans) arranged in a semicircular fashion, tuned to different pitches, with the performer sitting in the centre. It is played by striking the heads with the fingers of both the hands. The technique of playing the tabla tarang is different from that of the tabla. Due to the various pitches the heads of the tablas in the tabla tarang are tuned to, the performer can play different melodies and improvise.

Pakhawaj

The pakhawaj is supposed to be the original instrument from which the tabla was derived. It is a double-headed drum, which was also known as the mridanga (different from the mridangam). This was the drum used to accompany the dhrupad style of singing and the instruments that played in the dhrupad style.

It is a barrel-shaped drum with two heads made of layers of skin. The heads are stretched by leather straps, which run along the sides of the body over small cylindrical wooden tuning blocks. The

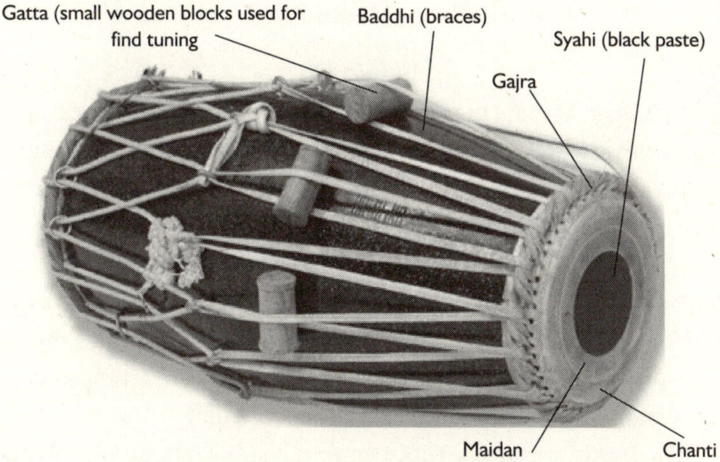

right head has a black spot (like the mridangam) and is tuned to the tonic. The tuning is done either by striking the rim of the head or by moving the cylindrical wooden blocks. The left head is the bass, to which a temporary paste of flour is normally applied just prior to playing, also like the mridangam. The drum is placed horizontally, either on the ground or the lap of the performer, and the left and right heads are played with the left and right hands respectively.

Nagara

These are a couple of cup-shaped kettledrums, traditional accompaniments to the shehnai. These drums, which are covered with stretched skin, are placed in front of the performer and usually played with a pair of sticks.

IDIOPHONES (MORE PERCUSSION)

Jalatarangam

Jalatarangam literally means water. This consists of a set of porcelain bowls of varying sizes. The bowls are arranged in a semicircular in front of the seated performer, in decreasing order in size, starting with the largest bowl to the performer's left and ending with the smallest one to his right. The bowls are filled with water and the pitch is changed by adjusting the volume of water in the bowl. The bigger bowls produce a deep, bass sound whereas the smaller ones produce high-pitch tones. Thus, the bowls are arranged in an increasing order of pitch from the left to the right.

The bowls are struck with two thin bamboo sticks, one held in each hand. All compositions of medium and fast tempi can be played effectively on this instrument.

Ghatam

The ghatam, an ancient south Indian percussion instrument, is a pot made of clay with brass, copper and iron filings. The mouth of the pot slants outward to form a ridge. The pitch of the ghatam depends on the size of the instrument, and minor tuning can be done by applying plasticine clay and water.

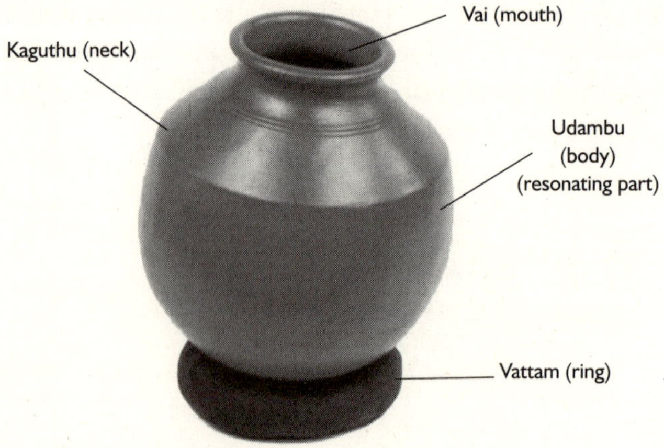

The performer sits cross-legged with the ghatam on his lap, the mouth of the instrument facing his belly. Hands, palms, fingers and also his nails are used to produce different sounds. At times, the ghatam is turned around, so that the mouth faces the audience, and the performer plays on the neck of the ghatam. It can also be moved to different positions while being played. Sometimes, the performer tosses the pot in the air and catches it, in rhythm, to the delight of the audience.

The ghatam can be played in a very fast tempo. It is a secondary percussion instrument that is normally played with the mridangam.

Morsing

Another secondary percussion instrument, the morsing is also sometimes called the moorchung.

It consists of a 'tongue' of springy metal, supported within a ring-like iron frame. The tongue is slightly curved at the free end and protrudes beyond the ring at the other end. It is held between the thumb and forefinger of the left hand and the narrow portion is inserted into the mouth. The curved end of the 'tongue' is plucked with the forefinger of the right hand. The cavity of the mouth serves as a resonator. A variety of sounds can be produced by the performer opening his mouth wider, decreasing the cavity of his mouth, controlling his breath and by manipulating his tongue. The instrument can be tuned by the application of wax to the tongue. The instrument has a nasal, twangy sound.

TRUMP PARTS

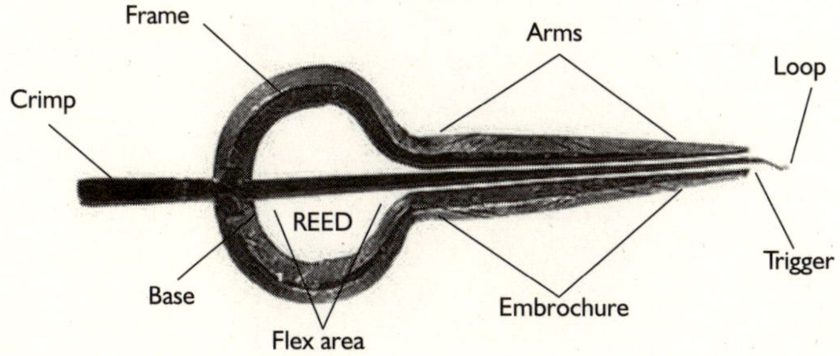

The above descriptions are of well-known and commonly heard instruments. Many of them had more ancient forms, which were subjected during Amir Khusrau's time to Persian influences and adapted to new uses. This trend of change and adaptation continues even today. In recent years, there have been modifications of some of the instruments by adding features like extra strings or an additional gourd or resonator. Hence there are slight variations between the different schools of performers. As time goes on, more changes and innovations can be expected.

Also, musically, to compensate for some of the limitations of certain instruments, for example, the inability to slide between notes in a struck instrument, artists have devised certain techniques to give an illusion of the desired ornamentation.

8

Musical Forms

The musical forms in south Indian music are all vocal forms, that is, all the compositions are written with words to be sung. The same compositions are also played on the various instruments.

The musical forms can be studied under two categories:

1. Abhyasa gana (abhyasa means 'practice' and gana means 'song')
2. Sabha gana (sabha means 'audience' or 'assembly').

In other words, forms that are designated for practice to improve one's technical skills (abhyasa gana) and those that are meant to be performed in front of an audience (sabha gana).

ABHYASA GANA

Gita or Gitam

Gitam literally means 'song'. It belongs to the abhyasa gana group. This is the first composition with words that one usually learns. It is a simple composition that has no divisions, performed in the same tempo from beginning to end with no melodic or rhythmic variations. The tune is very simple and based on a particular raga and tala. There are gitams in all the seven talas. For every swara there is usually a syllable of the words or a vowel extension. The lyrics are in praise of gods and goddesses. They are mostly composed in Sanskrit, Telugu or Kannada. There are two kinds of gitams:

1. Samanya gitam (samanya meaning 'common' or 'ordinary')
2. Lakshana gitam (lakshana meaning 'characteristics').

The samanya gitams are also known as sadharana gitams (sadharana meaning 'common') or sancari gitams (sancari meaning 'wandering' but here referring to 'commonly used'). The lakshana gitams give the lakshana or characteristics of the raga they are based on, for example, the notes used, the important notes, whether it is a parent or derived raga and so on.

Well-known composers of this form are Purandara Dasa, Paidala Gurumurti Sastrigal, Ramamatya and Venkatamakhi.

Swarajati

Swarajatis also belong to the abhyasa gana group and are learnt after gitams. They prepare the way for the varnam, a more complicated form. Similar to a varnam in structure, the swarajatis have three sections: the pallavi, the anupallavi and the charanams. Typically, the multiple charanams have different melodies that are first performed in swaras (sol-fa) and then repeated with the lyrics. Each charanam is performed in this manner before going on to the next. The lyrics are normally devotional in nature though, at times, they can contain a description of heroic deeds. Originally, the swarajati was a dance form containing jatis (rhythmic syllables). Later on, the jatis were excluded by Shyama Shastri who refined and perfected this form into what it is today.

Well-known composers of this form are Shyama Shastri, Paccimiriyam Adiyappayya and Swati Tirunal.

Jatiswaram

The jatiswaram belongs to the dance repertoire and is very similar to the swarajati. It consists of three sections: the pallavi, the anupallavi and the charanams, which were originally intended to be performed in jatis (rhythmic syllables). However, the jatiswaram is now performed entirely in swaras. In the swarajati, the emphasis is on the music, whereas in the jatiswaram the emphasis is on the rhythm. In the latter, rhythmic patterns are woven into the melody.

Varnam

Of the abhyasa gana group, the varnam is the most important. Varnams are erudite compositions. They contain not only all the important and appealing features of the raga but also all the unique and unusual phrases that are typical to a particular raga. Hence, it requires dexterity, knowledge, technique and good musicianship to compose good varnams.

The study and practice of varnams are of utmost importance both to the singer for voice-training and the instrumentalist for developing good fingering techniques. The swara passages are a good basis for the performer to learn the technique of swara-kalpana (improvisation based on the swaras). Practising the varnam at multiple speeds also gives one a good, steady sense of rhythm. The lyrics of the varnam are usually in praise of a deity or a patron.

Although the varnam belongs to the 'technical group', it is also performed in concerts, unlike the gitam, which is not performed. If a varnam is included, it is traditionally performed as the opening piece of the concert.

The varnam consists of two halves:

1. Purvanga or the first half
2. Uttaranga or the second half

The purvanga consists of three sections: the pallavi, the anupallavi and the chittai-swaras (also called muktayi-swaras). The uttaranga consists of the charanam and the ettugede-swaras (also called chittai-swaras). Both halves are almost equal in length.

The pallavi and the anupallavi are normally two lines (two rhythmic cycles) each, with lyrics. The chittai-swaras are passages of sol-fa syllables. One starts with the pallavi (normally performed twice) then goes on to the anupallavi (which is also performed twice), then on to the chittai-swara and then back to the pallavi. If the varnam is performed at multiple speeds, the first half is performed at all the speeds before going on to the second half.

The charanam is usually one line (one rhythmic cycle) with lyrics. The ettugede-swaras are groups of swara passages. There are normally four or more groups of ettugede-swaras. The first group of swaras is usually one rhythmic cycle and is made up of long notes. The next group is usually also one cycle long, the third and fourth are two and four cycles long, respectively. In some varnams, the last group can be longer. The charanam is used as a theme of return, that is, after each group of swaras, one returns to the charanam line before going on to the next swara group. If the swaras are to be performed at different speeds, each group is performed at the different speeds along with the charanam line before going on to the next group.

There are two kinds of varnams:

1. Tana varnam
2. Pada varnam

The tana varnam is performed in music concerts and the pada varnam belongs to the dance repertoire. Pada varnams are normally performed at a slower tempo than the tana variants. This is because the varnam is used in dance to express bhavas (emotions). The tana varnam gets its name from the fact that it is developed in the tana style. Tana means 'to stretch' or 'to extend'. The tana varnam has more vowel extensions in the lyrics than the pada varnam. The lyrics in the tana varnam are generally in praise of a deity, or the guru, or a description of the particular varna, whereas in the pada varnam, the theme is generally shringara (aesthetic experience of love). This similarity to the padam form is what gave this type of varnam its name. In the tana varnam, only the pallavi, anupallavi and the charanam have lyrics, whereas in the pada varnam all sections have lyrics. In the latter, the chittai-swaras and the ettugede-swaras are first performed in swaras and then repeated with the lyrics. The swara passages are usually accompanied by nritta (pure dance movements) and the passages with the lyrics are normally accompanied by abhinaya (expression of some sentiment or passion by looks, gestures, postures). Some pada varnams also have jatis or solkattus (drum syllables) incorporated in them.

The varnam is the last type of abhyasa gana that is learned before going on to the kriti form. The varnam is supposed to be practised in tri-kala or three speeds (the first speed, twice as fast, and double the second speed). In most cases, though, they are only performed in one or two speeds in concerts. It is to the credit of my father and guru, Professor V. Lakshminarayana that varnams later came to be performed at multiple speeds, using the concept of pancha-nadai, where every beat of a rhythmic cycle is subdivided into three, four, five, seven and nine pulses. Building on this concept, I recorded the popular Mohana varnam *'Ninnu kori'* in fifteen speeds along with the legendary mridangam genius Palghat Mani Iyer. I must also mention here that such a feat would have not been possible but for the innovative and masterful violin-playing techniques created by Professor Lakshminarayana.[1]

Well-known composers are Paccimiriyam Adiyappayya, Pallavi Gopala Iyer, Veena Kuppayyar, Patnam Subramania Iyer and Ramnad Srinivasa Iyengar.

SABHA GANA

Kriti

The kriti is the most important form belonging to the sabha gana group. Kritis form the major part of all existing musical compositions. Normally, there is no concert without a kriti in it. A kriti is a composition based on a particular raga and a particular tala. The composer is not too restricted in the sense that he can choose the

[1] I have composed a pancha-nadai varnam in Kannada to showcase all the different nadais in the same varnam.

raga, tala, speed, style and text that he wants and can concentrate on bringing out the beauty and the feeling of the raga. Kritis are suitable for neraval and swara-kalpana improvisations (see the segment on Ragam-Tanam-Pallavi for details).

The kriti evolved from the older form, the kirtana, which was in vogue around the fourteenth century. With its evolution, many of the older forms became outdated. In the kirtana, the emphasis is more on the sahitya or text, mostly devotional. In the kriti, though almost always devotional in nature, it can also be secular. The emphasis is more on musicality and aesthetic content, the music being more complex than in the kirtana form.

The kriti has three sections: the pallavi, the anupallavi and the charanam. The performer starts with the pallavi, sings it with melodic variations, known as sangatis, then goes to the anupallavi, which is also performed with variations and returns to the pallavi before going to the final section. Typically, the pallavi and the anupallavi each have two lines of text, whereas the charanam is twice as long. The music of the second half of the charanam is usually the same as that of the anupallavi, though the text is different. In the charanam one usually finds the mudra. Literally meaning 'stamp', this is the signature each composer uses to mark or stamp the composition as his own. Tyagaraja used his own name (he was named after the presiding deity at Tiruvarur), Dikshitar used Guruguha, Shyama Shastri used Shyamakrishna, and so on.

Some variations on the kriti form:

1. Generally, in the kritis of Muthuswami Dikshitar the anupallavi and the second half of the charanam do not have the same tune. In fact, some of his shorter compositions have only the first two sections, the pallavi and the anupallavi. In these compositions, the second section is called the samashti charanam (samashti meaning 'aggregate' or 'totality'), that is, a combination of the anupallavi and the charanam.
2. Some of Tyagaraja's kritis have multiple charanams with different

dhatus (tunes). For example, his famous pancharatna-kritis in which the lines are first performed in sol-fa syllables and then repeated with the text, like the swarajati and the pada varnam.

3. Some kritis include chittai-swaras of sol-fa syllables.
4. Madhyama-kala sahitya (madhyama-kala meaning 'medium tempo' and sahitya meaning 'text') is typical of Muthuswami Dikshitar's kritis. It consists of a passage, with lyrics, which is double the tempo of the rest of the kriti.
5. Manipravala kritis where the sahitya is in two or more languages (Sanskrit and Telugu; Sanskrit, Telugu and Tamil) as opposed to the regular kriti where the text is entirely in one language. These were composed by composers who were well-versed in several languages like Swati Tirunal.

Padas or Padams

Padams are beautiful, scholarly compositions. In the past, the term 'pada' was used to denote any devotional song, but now it stands for a particular musical form which belongs to the realm of dance music. Though the padam belongs to the dance repertoire, it is also sung or played in concerts due to its excellent musical quality. Padams bring out the essence of the emotion of the raga. This form was perfected in the seventeenth century by the composer Kshetrajna who is rightly known as the father of the modern padam. Like the kriti, the padam has three sections: the pallavi, anupallavi and charanam. It may have three or more charanams, which have the same melody but vary in text. It is usually performed in a slower tempo. The text generally deals with the concept of the nayaka-nayaki bhava. The most common emotions that one comes across in the padams are: yearning in love, the trials and tribulations of love, the hopes, frustrations and disappointments in the path of love, anger, jealousy and so on. These emotions make it the perfect vehicle for the dancer to perform abhinaya.

Padams are usually in Tamil or Telugu. The Telugu padams are usually in praise of Krishna whereas the Tamil padams are generally in praise of Subrahmanya (Muruga). The lyrics of the padams are often filled with shringara rasa.

Some well-known composers of padams are Kshetrajna, Sarangapani (Telugu), Ghanam Krishna Iyer and Subbarama Iyer (Tamil).

Javalis

The javali is a much lighter form compared to the padam, in its musical and emotional content. The javali evolved around the nineteenth century. Javalis deal with human relationships and are sensuous and erotic in content. The tunes are light, catchy and appealing, which makes them extremely popular. The lyrics are simple and colloquial, and often border on the obscene. Javalis are performed in concerts, usually towards the end, and also in dance concerts.

The word javali is derived from the word 'javadi', which means 'lewd poetry' in Kannada. They are usually in Kannada or Telugu. The lyrics deal with emotions like infidelity and jealousy. Javalis lack the dignity of the padam and its sublimation of emotions. They are composed in light ragas like Kapi and Kamas. Often, the composer takes liberties with the ragas, introducing foreign notes and embellishments to enhance the composition. The javali too has three sections: pallavi, anupallavi and charanam. Some javalis have more than one charanam having the same tune.

Some prominent composers of this form are Dharmapuri Subbarayar, Swati Tirunal and Ramnad Srinivasa Iyengar.

Tillana

Tillanas are short, lively and invigorating compositions. This is another form that belongs to dance music, but performed in a music concert towards the end. The tillana consists of three sections: pallavi, anupallavi and charanam. The pallavi and the anupallavi usually consist of swaras and jatis. The charanam has all the three: lyrics, swaras and jatis. The jatis include syllables like nadru, dhim, dire, na, ti, la, na and so on. The form derives its name from the syllables ti-la-na.

The great king-composer Swati Tirunal was the first to compose tillanas, in the nineteenth century. They are of two kinds: those that are sung or played in concerts and those performed in dance concerts. In the former, there is more emphasis on the raga and they are performed at a faster tempo. The latter are performed in medium tempo and the jatis are worked into the composition so that they allow the dancer to exhibit variations in footwork.

Tillanas are most commonly set in talas like Adi or Rupaka. The text may be in Sanskrit, Telugu, or Tamil.[2]

Well-known composers of this form are Swati Tirunal, Patnam Subramania Iyer, Ramnad Srinivasa Iyengar and Mysore Sadashiva Rao.

Tiruppugazh

Tiruppugazh, meaning 'praise of the Lord', is the name given to a group of devotional songs in Tamil composed by the saint-poet Arunagirinathar. His mudra or signature word is Perumal. Often sung or played at the end of the concert, tiruppugazh lyrics are tuned in traditional ragas and occasionally set to very unusual time cycles that are based on the poetic metre of the verse.

Ragam-Tanam-Pallavi

This is an extremely complicated and involved form which is performed in the latter part of the concert. The pallavi, which consists of a single line of composition, is the only pre-composed part. The rest of it is completely improvised. Hence, it is a very demanding and challenging form, both technically and musically, where all the different aspects of one's musicianship are put to the test. The ragam portion challenges the performer's creative capacity in the detailed

[2] Based on the pancha-nadai concept, I composed a tillana in Vasanta that uses all the five nadais along with other rhythmic syllables.

unfolding of the raga. The tanam is a free improvisation with a rhythmic structure to it, challenging the creativity of the musician. The pallavi is a challenge to his ability to improvise with complex and intricate patterns. Hence, the performer must have good technique, a deep knowledge of the rules of the raga and a good command over the intricate rhythmic patterns of tala. In a concert, if the musician performs a ragam-tanam-pallavi, then the most elaborate raga exposition is done here.

This form consists of three parts:

Ragam

In this section, the performer freely improvises on a particular raga, without any rhythmic accompaniment. The performer elaborately develops the raga in stages, maintaining all its rules and staying within the strict framework. As mentioned earlier, the performer is free to improvise, but there are also some guidelines which restrict him. For example, a raga is traditionally based on a scale of five, six or seven notes and, of these, there are some notes that are more important than the others (vadi and samvadi). They have to be stressed more than the others while improvising. The performer cannot use any notes that do not belong to the raga and, if any of the notes are microtones, they must be used. The ragam portion starts slowly, bringing out the charm, appeal and intrinsic mood of the raga. This is systematically built up in speed and intensity ending with pharans (fast passages), which allow the performer to exhibit his technical virtuosity.

Tanam

This is the second section of the ragam-tanam-pallavi and is only associated with this musical form.[3] The syllables a, nom, da, tha and

[3] The only exception being veena concerts where the vainika might play a raga alapana, followed by tanam, and then a kriti after that. The reason for this being that the tanam form is particularly suited to the veena, and perhaps even evolved from veena-playing.

so on, are used while improvising; there is no lyrical content. The improvisation is typically without any rhythmic accompaniment. Though there is no percussion accompaniment, the performer introduces the element of rhythmic pulses into his improvisation. At the end of each phrase, a recognisably typical rhythmic cadence (pattern) is used to indicate the end of that section.

Pallavi

The third section consists of a single line composition of the lyric, which is usually set to a single cycle of tala (except in the case of talas like Chapu and short talas like Rupaka). The lyrics may be devotional or secular in content and may be in any language. The word pallavi is derived from the three syllables pa-la-vi: **pa**dam (words), **la**ya (rhythm) and **vi**nyasam (variations). The pallavi is referred to in Sarangadeva's thirteenth-century text *Sangita Ratnakara* but it did not evolve till the eighteenth century. The pallavi is performed, without variations, two or three times for the percussionist to familiarise himself with it so that he can accompany the melody line, because this is where the percussion starts playing.

Here are some of the main features of the pallavi:

1. **Neraval:** Literally meaning 'filling up' or 'spreading out', the neraval consists of filling up portions of the pallavi line with new, creative melodic ideas. The performer improvises new melodies around the lyrics of the pallavi, but keeps the rhythmic structure constant. This type of improvisation is also used in the kriti where one line of the kriti is taken and used as the theme for the neraval.
2. **Trikalam** (tri meaning 'three' and kalam meaning 'speed' or 'tempo'): In this section, the pallavi line is performed in three tempi, keeping the tala constant. The first is a slow speed, the second is twice as fast and the third is twice as fast as the second speed. Sometimes, the trikala is done the other way around. The first is a medium speed, the second is half the first speed

and the third is half the second speed. Sometimes the pallavi is performed by changing the nadai from four pulses per beat to three.

3. **Swara-kalpana** (swara meaning 'sol-fa syllable' or 'note' and kalpana meaning 'imagination'): This consists of improvisations based on swaras in medium and fast speeds. After each passage or section of swara-kalpana, the performer returns to the pallavi line. This type of improvisation depends upon the performer's technical and musical ability. The concept of nadais can be used effectively to bring rhythmic variations in the pallavi.
4. **Ragamalika:** The pallavi often ends with this section which literally means 'garland of ragas'. The performer improvises in a variety of ragas and, at the end of each raga section, comes back to the rhythmic theme of the original pallavi, which is performed either in the original raga (of the ragam-tanam-pallavi) or in each of the ragas of the ragamalika.

Tani Avartanam

Though the tani avartanam is not a separate musical form, it forms an important part of the concert mode. This refers to the solo playing of the percussionists. The main artist normally allows the percussionist(s) to perform a solo, either after performing a major composition (kriti) or as a part of the ragam-tanam-pallavi. In some cases, he may also play a short, simple kriti in the Adi tala and give the percussionist a solo.

Basically, the percussionist plays in the same tala of the composition performed by the soloist. When the solo is given after a major kriti or ragam-tanam-pallavi, it usually follows the neraval and swara-kalpana. The percussionist is expected to improvise and return, after each section of improvisation, to the starting point (eduppu) of the melodic line of the composition that is selected for the neraval and swara-kalpana improvisation. Sometimes, even before the neraval and swara-kalpana, the percussionist is given space to repeat the trikala improvisation of the main performer. The percussionist has the freedom to play anything he wants within the framework of the tala and the established tempo.

The solo can broadly be divided into three stages leading to the finale. In the opening stages, the percussionist starts playing rhythmic phrases in a slower tempo, leading to medium tempo patterns. He also plays moras that are pre-composed rhythmic structures which extend over four or more cycles of rhythm. It is not uncommon to play some korvais which are also pre-composed, cadence-like patterns repeated three times to lead to the eduppu and then to the next section. In the middle section, some percussionists play one or more nadais and here also moras and korvais are played. Then, one comes back to the original nadai, leading to the third section where fast passages are played to show the percussionist's virtuosity and technical capability. This leads to the finale where a long mora is played (normally extending for four cycles of rhythm in the case of the Adi tala) ending with a korvai, which is repeated three times leading to the eduppu, where the main artist comes in again, with the beginning of the composition, to indicate the completion of the tani avartanam. This is the general description of the tani (as it is called) but it varies a great deal from artist to artist. This format has been established only in the past few decades.

The primary percussion is provided by the mridangam (except the nagaswaram which is accompanied by the tavil). When there is more than one percussion accompaniment, the mridangam player leads the solo. After he finishes a section, the others (ghatam, khanjira, morsing) take turns in a definite order of succession and try to follow the same (or similar) rhythmic structure and patterns, in addition to exhibiting their own skills and virtuosity. This is followed by the middle section, where they might play different nadais. Once again, the secondary percussionists normally play only the nadais played by the main percussionist. In the third section, they play fast virtuoso passages, taking turns. Here they do a koraippu (meaning 'reduction' in Tamil) where the length of each turn gets shorter and shorter. For example, the mridangam player may start with a four-cycle turn, followed by the others also playing the same length, and then decrease it to two cycles, one cycle, half-cycle, quarter-cycle and so on. This is made into an exciting and interesting portion, leading to the final mora and korvai where the main performer joins in and ends the solo section.

It is also very interesting when, in addition to the secondary percussions, a vocal percussion (konnakol) is also added to the ensemble. When the ensemble is made up of leading exponents in their field who are not overawed by one another, especially the mridangam player, the effect can be spectacular.

On many occasions, I have performed a trade-off with the percussionists during the final swara-kalpana—after I play a few rhythmic cycles of solfège improvisation, the mridangam player (or tavil player) plays a solo for the exact same number of cycles; then I play a few more cycles of improvisation and this is followed by a khanjira or ghatam solo; then I play a few more cycles of improvisation and this is followed by a morsing solo. This creates the effect of a musical conversation and gives a remarkable finale to the piece.

North Indian Musical Forms

The musical forms in north Indian music are divided into vocal forms and instrumental forms.

MUSICAL FORMS (VOCAL)

Dhrupad

It is believed that the dhrupad or Dhruvapada originated in the fifteenth century in Gwalior during the reign of Raja Mansingh Tomar. There are few exponents of this style today. The language of the lyrics is usually Sanskrit or Braj. This style of singing is grand and heavy, making it, therefore, more suitable to the male voice. The rasas (aesthetic experiences) predominant in this style of singing are vira (heroic), shringara (romantic) and shanta (peaceful). The dhrupad typically has four sections: sthayi, antara, sanchari and abhog.

The sthayi is a melodic stanza that uses the first four notes of the madhya-sthayi (middle octave) and some of the notes from the mandra-sthayi (lower octave). The antara is a melodic stanza that uses the second half of the madhya-sthayi and some of the notes of the tara-sthayi (upper octave). The sanchari is the part where the raga is methodically developed, building on what has already been performed during the sthayi and antara segments; this melodic portion uses notes from all three octaves. The abhog is the finale that goes back to the melodic motifs developed in the sthayi, along with certain rhythmic variations. In some traditions, the third part is abhog and the concluding section is the sanchari.

There are four different styles of the dhrupad: 1. Gauhar vani, 2. Khandar vani, 3. Dagar vani, and 4. Nohar vani, each with its own special characteristics and approach. These are roughly linked to the five gitis (performing styles): Shuddha, Bhinna, Gaura, Vegasvara and Sadharani.

Talas commonly used in this style are Chautal (twelve beats), Tivratal (seven beats), Jhaptal (ten beats) and Dhamartal (fourteen beats). In this style, dugan (second speed), chaugan (third speed; double the second speed), bol-taan (singing the melody with lyrics) and gamakas (musical embellishments) are used, but not taans (singing the melody without lyrics, using notes or akara, which is the sound 'a').

As the popularity of the khyal style increased, it replaced the dhrupad more and more.

Dhamar

Dhamars are compositions, similar to the dhrupads but not as grave. They are set to the Dhamar tala of fourteen beats. The lyrics are usually descriptions of the Holi festival and the pranks of Krishna who showers the gopis (cow-girls) with powders and paints of many colours.

Khyal

Khyal, in Persian, means 'thought' or 'imagination'. It is the most popular north Indian classical vocal form today. It is a short composition based on a raga, set to a particular tala: Ektal (twelve beats), Jhumra (fourteen beats), Rupak (seven beats), Jhaptal (ten beats) and Teental (sixteen beats) being the most common. The mood is generally romantic or devotional. It is not as rigid as the dhrupad.

There are two types of khyals, the bada (big) or vilambit khyal, and the chota (small) or drut khyal. The vilambit is the slow khyal, which is performed first. The drut is faster and performed in the latter part. Both khyals have two sections: sthayi (or asthayi) and antara. The sthayi is usually performed in the lower or middle range of the octave and the antara in the middle and upper range of the octave.

The khyal emerged around the fifteenth century. Some people believe that Amir Khusrau created this form. Another name associated with the khyal is that of Sultan Hussain Sharqi. However, the best-known composers of the khyal were two singers, Sadarang and Adarang (who lived in the early eighteenth century during the reign of Mohammad Shah Rangile). They composed thousands of khyals and propagated them through their numerous students.

The vilambit khyal composition is followed by a detailed delineation of the raga. This usually starts out in the lower range of the octave and slowly builds up to the higher octave and also in tempo. At the end of an improvisational passage, one comes back to the beginning of the khyal and ends on the downbeat (sam). Other forms of improvisation used are bol-taans, sargams and taans. The vilambit starts out slow and is gradually sped up towards the end. After the vilambit, the drut khyal is performed. This composition is much faster than the vilambit khyal. Fast taan patterns, sometimes sargams, are performed keeping the first line of the composition as the theme of return. The tempo of the fast khyal may vary from a medium to a very fast one.

Ṭappa

The tappa came from the Punjab and was the song of the camel-drivers. It is usually composed in Punjabi. This is a fast and lively piece with many swift tans. This form is said to have been created by Shori Miyan who lived in the court of Asaf-ud-Daula in Lucknow. It is considered a light piece and composed in ragas like Kafi, Jhinjhoti, Bhairavi, Khamaj and so on. It consists of two halves: the asthayi and the antara.

Thumri

The thumri is a light classical form. It is usually performed in ragas like Desh, Khamaj, Pilu, Bhairavi, Pahadi and so on. It is less rigid than the khyal, and allows for a lot of artistic and creative freedom. In this form the performer has the license to occasionally use notes that do not belong to the raga. It is usually performed in a medium tempo and also consists of an asthayi and an antara. The themes deal with love, particularly of the maidens' pining for Krishna. This form originated in the courts of the Nawabs of Lucknow. There are two famous styles of thumri singing—the purab ang or eastern style and the pashcim ang or the western style. The purab ang includes the Lucknow and Benares styles and the pashcim ang is the Punjab style. The purab ang is slow, elaborate and richly emotional, whereas in the pashcim ang, the emphasis is on creative virtuosity. The latter is a more popular, sensuous style where much importance is given to clarity and to the emotional enunciation of the lyric. The talas normally used are Dadra, Keherva and Deepchandi.

Tarana

Taranas are compositions consisting of meaningless words or syllables like ta, na, dere, dani, dhim. They are based on ragas sung in khyals and normally performed either in place of, or after, the fast khyal. It is believed that when Amir Khusrau came to India, he was worried as all the compositions were in Sanskrit. He knew only Persian and

Arabic, so he set meaningless sound-syllables and Persian words to ragas and this became a new form known as the tarana. This form also has two sections: asthayi and antara, performed usually in the medium-fast to fast tempo range.

Ghazal

Ghazals are love poems, usually in Urdu, set to music. Considered to be light numbers, words play an important part in ghazals, which are not necessarily set to any strict raga, nor do they have traditional tunes. A ghazal may be performed in several different tunes. It consists of couplets dealing with love, pining, betrayal and fidelity, or are philosophical in content. The words are of utmost importance in a ghazal which has become a popular form today.

Bhajan

Bhajans are devotional songs that are set to music. Like ghazals, they are considered to be light music and do not have to be confined to a particular raga. They may be performed in several different tunes in praise of deities. Bhajans composed by the saint-poets of the sixteenth century like Mirabai, Tulsidas, Surdas and Kabirdas are popular even today.

MUSICAL FORMS (INSTRUMENTAL)

Alap, Jod, Jhala

This is the form basically followed by instruments for the raga improvisation. It corresponds closely to the ragam-tanam improvisation in south Indian classical music.

Alap begins with the slow improvisation of the chosen raga. Even though the improvisation is free, one is still bound by all the strict rules that govern the raga. There is no rhythmic accompaniment.

Jod is also free improvisation but with the added element of rhythm. There is still no rhythmic accompaniment, but there are rhythmic cadences used in the improvisation.

Jhala is the culmination of the improvisation built up in speed and intensity, still without any rhythmic accompaniment.

Gat

Gats are compositions for instruments. They are set to definite ragas and talas and have two sections like the khyal asthayi and antara. Like the khyal there are two kinds of gats: vilambit (slow) and drut (fast).

Dhun

Dhuns or tunes are light classical compositions for instruments. They are usually in light ragas like Khamaj, Pilu, Desh and allow for the mixing of ragas as does the thumri form.

Appendix

INDIAN MUSIC COMPOSERS

A composer in the Indian tradition is very different from his Western counterpart. Many of the leading composers in the Carnatic tradition were saints and led a strict, spiritually disciplined life. Most of their compositions were in praise of gods and goddesses. The composers who travelled to pilgrimage areas sang spontaneously there. These compositions were sacred rather than secular in content, and were written as a musical offering and prayer to deities (not with the intention of performing). Some composers refused patronage from kings since they did not believe in singing in praise of men. Since there were no formal schools or teachers to teach compositions as there were in the Western contexts, these composers learnt music from other learned musicians and then developed their own style and approach. Some of them composed in many languages. They were well-versed in the epics (like the Ramayana and the Mahabharata), drawing on them for the subject matter of their songs.

While the prominent composers have been discussed in the first chapter, here are some of the other important composers in the tradition—

Jayadeva (twelfth century CE) is widely known for his poem, *Gita Govinda.* It is an important work of art in the bhakti tradition, and contains poems known as ashta-padis (literally, 'eight steps') since each segment has eight verses. There are mangala-slokas at the end of all the hymns. The twenty-four songs have been translated into many languages. Even the place Jayadevapura got its name as Jayadeva began and completed all his compositions there.

Jayadeva made the dashaavataara (ten incarnations of Vishnu) concept famous through one of the verses of the *Gita Govinda*. The famous tribhangi stance (crossing the legs) of Krishna playing the flute was also made popular by him.

He was responsible for laying the foundation of literature in modern Odia and other languages, since his language was simple and easily understandable by the public. He tweaked his poetry and experimented with his lyrical compositions so that they could be easily adapted into music and dance forms.

Jayadeva institutionalised the devadasi (women dancers who were dedicated to the temple deity) system in Odia temples. Thanks to his works, the temples in Odia dedicated a separate dance hall within the temple to the Mahari dancers—called the Natamandira. The ashta-padis composed by Jayadeva continue to remain popular and have been translated into many different languages.

Mirabai was a sixteenth century Hindu mystic, poet and devotee of Krishna. She was a Rajput princess, educated in music and religion as well as in politics and government affairs. During her childhood, an image of Krishna was given to her by a holy man. From then on, she became an ardent worshiper of Krishna. She is a celebrated Bhakti saint in the north Indian Hindu tradition.

At the time, India's devotional poets expressed their love for God via different analogies—for example, the love between a mother and her child. Mirabai belonged to this tradition, and gained widespread popularity because her bhajans used easily understandable lyrics and relatable, everyday images.

Mirabai composed primarily in two languages—Rajasthani and Braj Bhasa. She is credited with the creation of a unique raga—

Mira's Malhar. Her verses were called padas, and her devotional poems were called bhajans. Between four hundred and one thousand three hundred of her compositions have survived, and have been translated into Hindi, Gujarathi and Rajasthani. Even in a time of spiritual decline and prevailing war conditions, Mirabai's life served as an example of devotion and pure love for God.

Chaitanya Mahaprabhu, a fifteenth century Vedic spiritual leader, is believed to be an avatar of Lord Krishna. He is credited with founding Gaudiya Vaishnavism, the religious movement that advocates for the worship of Lord Vishnu. This movement preaches Bhakti yoga as a way to realise the ultimate truth.

Chaitanya Mahaprabhu was a child prodigy who became a scholar at a very young age. He is known for composing *Siksastakam*, a Sanskrit prayer containing eight verses. He is also credited with popularising the *Maha Mantra* or *Hare Krishna Mantra*. At a young age, Chaitanya Mahaprabhu had thousands of followers, and he even opened a school. He would perform along with his wife Vishnupriya; he sang while she danced. At the age of sixteen, he went to Gaya, where he preached, expressed various religious and devotional sentiments, sang, and danced. He is also credited for the introduction of the sankirtan—a path by which one can attain spiritual perfection by chanting the Lord's name.

Tulsidas, known for his devotion to Lord Rama, was a Hindu Vaishnava saint. He was also called Goswami Tulsidas and is believed to be an incarnation of Maharishi Valmiki, who wrote the original Ramayana. He is best known as the author of the epic *Ramcharitmanas,* which retells the story of Rama's life in the vernacular Awadhi dialect of Hindi.

Tulsidas started writing the *Ramcharitmanas* in the year 1631, and it took him over two years to complete it. He lived for a hundred and twenty-six years, and composed a total of twenty-two works.

Although he is a Sanskrit scholar, he is also considered one of the best Hindi poets.

Most of Tulsidas' poetry has been set to music and been sung, performed and recorded. Biographers have identitfied twelve works as his six major and six minor works. Besides these, he was also popular for Sanskrit and Awadhi compositions like the *Hanuman Chalisa*, *Hanuman Bahuk*, *Tulsi Satsai* and *Hanuman Ashtak*.

Narayana Teertha (1580–1660) authored the *Krishna Lila Tarangini*, a great dance drama in Sanskrit. He mastered music at a very young age, and became a sanyasi (renounced worldly life) early on. He was well versed in the Bhagavatam—one of the eighteen Puranas. (The Puranas are sacred works in Sanskrit which contain eighteen thousand verses and tell the story of the ten incarnations of Vishnu, including Krishna.)

The *Krishna Leela Tarangini* is an intriguing drama, as Narayana Teertha used songs, prose, shlokas, and couplets to tell the story. The *Krishna Lila Tarangini* tells the story of Krishna from his birth, ending with his marriage to Rukmini. Narayana Teertha passed away at the age of eighty in 1660.

Bhadrachala Ramadas (1620–1688), formerly named Gopanna, wrote songs in Sanskrit and Telugu. He was born in a small village in Andhra Pradesh. His deep devotion to Lord Rama earned him the title of Ramadas, which means one who serves Lord Rama.

Gopanna's parents both passed away when he was very young, so his uncles helped him find work. He was a revenue collector in the village of Bhadrachalam, where there was a Rama temple in desperate need of repair. Ramadas decided to rebuild the temple and adorn the deities with expensive jewellery. Initially, he was able to raise funds for this. However, when he was halfway through his project, he ran out of money and was unable to raise more. Finally, he had to use government money to finish rebuilding the temple.

For this, he served a prison sentence of twelve years. As the legend goes, Rama and Lakshmana appeared in human form at the end of his prison sentence, and paid off the money he took from the government.

Ramadas' songs contain more number of charanams, and he composed in the kirtana form. He used simple language and his music was very pleasing. Tyagaraja was impressed by Ramadas's devotion to Rama and praised him in a few of his compositions.

Arunachala Kavirayar (1711–1788) was the author of the first Tamil musical drama, *Rama Natakam.* He was born in 1711, in Tilliyadi in the Thanjavur district in Tamil Nadu. He was well versed in Sanskrit, Tamil and Telugu. The lyrics of *Rama Natakam* were written by him but the music was composed by his disciples Kothandarama lyer and Venkatarama lyer. This drama is a promiment example of such a composition—where the lyrics and music are authored by different people.

Rama Natakam told the story of Ramayana in the form of a story-song or darus. The ragas he chose accurately expressed the emotions of his songs, and he generously used Tamil proverbs and popular sayings in his work. *Rama Natakam* was first performed at the Srirangam temple and it soon gained a lot of popularity. It was universally loved by people since it told the story of the well-known epic, Ramayana and its songs were simple.

Kavirayar was acknowledged by some of the great patrons of his time: the king of Ranjore, Rulaja Maharaja and others. His other popular works include *Sirkazhi Sthata Puranam*, *Sirkazhi Kovai, Hanumar Pillai* and *Ajomukhi Nataka.*

Veena Kuppayyar (1798–1860) was born in Tiruvotriyur near Madras. He is best known as Tyagaraja's most successful disciple, who outperformed the other disciples in the art of composing. Veena Kuppayyar learnt to play the veena from his father Sambamurti Shastri—a celebrated veena player of the time. He composed various kritis, ranging from simple to extremely complex and used the mudra Gopala Dasa. He lived with Tyagaraja for many years, perfecting his form. Of his works, his tanavarnams are best known. His son, Tiruvotriyur Tyagayyar, was also a well-known composer.

Pacchimiriam Adiyappa (eighteenth century CE) was a great veena player who composed several kritis and varnams. Viriboni, his varnam composed in raga Bhairavi, is one of his more popular works. He used the mudra Sri Venkatarama in his compositions. He was widely appreciated and was a State musician in the Thanjavur court. He received the title of Tana Varna Marga Darsi (guide to the tanavarna). Many of his disciples went on to become legends in their own right, like Shyama Shastri and Ghanam Krishna Iyer.

Sadashiva Brahmendra was an eighteenth century scholar who wrote devotional songs in Sanskrit. He was born in Tiruvisainallur, near Kumbakonam and initially studied from Ramabhadra Dikshitar. He then went on to learn from the Shankaracharya in Kanchipuram. Some of his works include *Brahma Sutra Viruddi*, *Atma Vidya Vilasam* and *Siva Manasika Puja* kirtanas. Sadashiva Brahmendra used the mudras paramahamsa or hamsa. His compositions are simple but contain deep philosophical ideas. His admirers find the beauty in the simplicity of his compositions. In the last years of his life, he took a vow of silence. He is said to have performed many miracles and there are several stories that talk of these miracles.

Gopalakrishna Bharati (1811–1896) was born in the Thanjavur district of Tamil Nadu. His parents passed away when he was very young. He learnt the Vedas from the scholar, Govinda Yati. He was also proficient in Hindustani music. The Tamil musical drama *Nandanar Charitram* was his greatest contribution. This musical drama deals with the story of the Shaivite saint Nandanar. Bharati's poetic genius, his expertise in portraying the various characters and his masterful command of music make the work a masterpiece.

Ghanam Krishna Iyer (nineteenth century), the youngest son of Ramaswamy lyer, was born near Trichy in Tamil Nadu. He was a student of the famous composer, Pacchimiriam Adiyappa. He also studied with Bobbili Kesavayya. His padams in Tamil are great contributions to Carnatic music. They are full of beautiful music and soul-stirring emotions. They lend themselves well to abhinaya (expression of some sentiment, or passion, by looks, gestures and postures) in dance concerts. He used Subramania, Muthukumara, Velava and other names of Subramaniam as his mudra in his compositions. He met great composers like Tyagaraja and Gopalakrishna Bharati during his lifetime. He was honored by many kings and patrons.

Subbarama Dikshitar (1839–1906) was the last well-known name in the Dikshitar family. He was the grandson of Baluswami Dikshitar, brother of Muthuswami Dikshitar. From the age of five, he was trained in music as well as Sanskrit and Telugu. He learnt to play the veena from his father. He was also taught sacred literature and the theoretical aspects of music. At the age of ten, he is said to have composed a varnam which he sang for the king of Ettayapuram. The audience thought it was composed by his father. The king himself was rather skeptical and asked him to compose a jatiswaram with certain specifications within an hour. The young genius finished composing it in forty-five minutes. The king was extremely pleased and showered him with gifts. Subbarama Dikshitar composed several other varnams, kritis, ragamalikas and more.

Besides being a gifted composer, he was also an eminent musicologist whose contribution is monumental. He wrote a work called *Sangita Sampradaya Pradarshini*, in Telugu, which was published in the year 1904. This work contains not only all his compositions but also Venkatamakhi's theory of music and the compositions of Muthuswami Dikshitar. This work was invaluable to musicologists and scholars who came after him. It also served as a guide in the publication of the kritis of Muthuswami Dikshitar.

Maha Vaidyanatha Iyer (1844–1893), born in Vaiyacheri near Thanjavur, was a great composer and a brilliant performer. He started learning music from Anayya. Later, he learnt music from Manambuchavadi Venkatasubbayyar, Tyagaraja's disciple.

Possessing a brilliant voice with a wide range, it is said he took great care to preserve it. He did not talk too much, did not eat spicy food and his disciples learnt music from his brother, Ramaswami Sivan, who was also a singer. He was given the title of Maha (great) at the tender age of twelve, making him the youngest musician to earn a title. When he was seven years old, he was able to improvise on a pallavi and also sing a raga alapana. At the age of ten, he started singing concerts with his brother. His forte was being able to sing long, detailed raga alapanas (improvisations) on even rare and uncommon ragas.

He was a brilliant composer who composed varnams, kritis and tillanas. His tillana in raga Kanada is the only one in the Simhanandana Tala (the longest of the one hundred and eight talas). His ragamalika on the seventy-two melakartas is his masterpiece. He used the mudra Guhadasa in his compositions.

Dharmapuri Subbarayar (nineteenth century) is the most notable composer of the Javali form. He lived in the second half of the nineteenth century. He has more javalis to his credit than other compositions. His javalis are brilliant and invigorating. The music is brisk, enjoyable and highly appealing. He used the mudra Dharmapurisa in his javalis.

Mysore Sadashiva Rao (nineteenth century) was a prominent composer from the court of Mysore in Karnataka. He was born in Chittoor and his father was Ganesha Rao. He came from a rich and noble family. He had several disciples who were well-known themselves. He learnt music from Walajapet Venkataramana Bhagavatar. He spent all his money on charity and in the service of God. Eventually, he became very poor. One of the foremost musicians of his day, he visited all the holy places in South India and composed kritis in praise of the various deities.

In one of his compositions, he describes Tyagaraja's visit to the palace in Walajapet which he was fortunate to have witnessed. He composed in Sanskrit and Telugu and his kritis are in madhyama kala (medium tempo). Besides kritis, he also composed varnams and tillanas. Of the several compositions that he wrote, only a few are now available.

Nilakantha Sivan (1839–1900) is a lesser-known Carnatic music composer. He did not receive any formal musical training, but his compositions exhibit technical brilliance. He was born in 1839 to Subramanya Iyer and Alagammal at Vadiveeswaram, a part of Nagercoil. He lived in Padmanabhapuram, the capital of the old Travancore. His father was an official in Nilakanthaswami temple at Padmanabhapuram. He worked as a village magistrate for more than a decade and then left his profession to take up religious practices full-time. Nilakantha Sivan composed close to fifteen hundred verses in one hundred and fifty compositions primarily to guide the common listeners to tread the spiritual path. He went by the name Nilakantha Dasan, after the main deity at Padmanabhapuram, Kerala. Nilakantha Sivan was invited to the courts of the kings of Travancore, Kochi, Ramanathapuram and Pudukkottai, and was given many honors.

His innate mysticism was probably awakened when he encountered Kodaganallur Sundara Swamigal. Sivan was not just a good singer; he was adept at giving musical discourses as well. Papanasam Sivan, who was part of the many bhajana goshtis (singing troupes who primarily sing devotional songs), was one of his prominent disciples. *Shambo Mahadeva Saranam* (Bauli), *Ananda Nadamaaduvaar Thillai* (Purvikalyani), *Enraikku Sivakirupai Varumo* (Mukhari), *Enna Vanthalum* (Kambhoji), *Oru Naal Oru Pozhuthakilum* (Kamas), *Vaa Vaa Kalaimathi* (Shankarabharanam),

Oraru Mugane (Ritigaula), *Kadaikkan Paaraiyya* (Darbar), and *Sivanai Ninaithu* (Kambhoji) are some of his popular compositions in Tamil.

Patnam Subramania Iyer (1845–1902) was not only a great composer but also a great performer. His guru was Manambuchavadi Venkatasubbayyar who was a disciple of Tyagaraja. He was very well-known and honored by several patrons and kings for his great talent. His compositions, which total around a hundred, include kritis, tana varnams, pada varnams, javalis and tillanas. Most of his compositions are in Telugu, but he also wrote in Sanskrit and Tamil. He had a superb style that reveals his genius as a composer. His compositions are extremely popular and are performed a lot. He used the mudra Venkateswara, Varada Venkateswara and slight variations of the two.

Tiruvottriyur Tyagayyar (1845–1917) was the son of the famous composer Veena Kuppayyar. Tyagayyar was an accomplished musician and a brilliant composer just like his father. He composed beautiful varnams, kritis and ragamalikas mainly in the Telugu language. Coimbatore Thayi is one of his renowned disciples.

Tyagayyar was famous for composing some of the most exquisite varnams in Carnatic music. Some of his renowned varnams are *Chalamela* (raga Darbar), *Ento Premato* (raga Surutti), *Intamodi Seya* (raga Saaranga), *Kamakshi Ninne* (raga Yadukula Kambhoji), *Karunimpa* (raga Sahana), *Sami Dayajuda* (raga Kedaragaula) and *Sami Ni Pai* (raga Ananda Bhairavi). Apart from this, he has composed varnams in ragas such as Pantuvarali, Kalyani, Kharaharapriya, Varali, Vasanta, Nattai, Saveri, Mukhari, Dhanyasi, Kedaram, Mohana, Manirangu and Madhyamavati.

Ramnad Srinivasa Iyenger (1860–1919) born in Ramnad, Tamil Nadu, to Narayana lyengar and Lakshmi Ammal. Iyengar was a disciple of Patnam Subramania lyer and accompanied his guru in his concerts. He soon became well-known and travelled a lot. He composed several kritis, varnams, javalis and tillanas like his teacher. He has composed in unusual ragas (e.g. Vamam in Varali) and talas (a tillana in one of the one hundred and eight talas). His compositions are popular even today. He used his name Srinivasa as his mudra in his compositions. He was also affectionately known as Poochchi lyengar ('poochchi' means insect).

Koteeswara Iyer (1869–1938) was one of the first artists to compose in all seventy-two melakarta ragas. He was the grandson of Kavi Kunjara Bharathi (1810–96), and took the mudra Kavi Kunjara Dasan in his honour. He was born to Nagarathinam Iyer, an illustrious musician himself. He was a vidwan of the Sivaganga Samasthanam. His ancestors lived in Tirunelveli and later moved to Prungarai in Ramanathapuram district.

Koteeswara Iyer studied music under Patnam Subramania Iyer and Ramnad Srinivasa Iyengar. He composed mainly in the Tamil language. While he was still a BA (English) student in Trichy, he started performing in small concerts, primarily singing Kavi Kunjara Bharathi's compositions. Devotional singers K Somasundaram and K Veeramani were his grandsons.

Mysore C. Rangaiah (1895–1984) was a vīṇā vidvān who hailed from Mysore. He was a disciple of Veena Shivaramiah, Chikka Subba Rao, and Veena Venkatagiriyappa. He had advanced training under Mysore Vasudevacharya. He has composed several varṇams and kṛitis as well as three operas (including one on the Rāmāyaṇa in twenty ragas). His compositions are in Kannada and Sanskrit. He composed kṛitis in all seventy-two melakarta ragas.

M. Balamurakikrishna (1930–2016) was an Indian Carnatic vocalist, musician, multi-instrumentalist, playback singer, composer and character actor. Known for the optimism and clarity of his three-octave vocals, Balamuralikrishna's musical journey has been characterised by his non-conformism, spirit of experimentation and boundless creativity. Balamuralikrishna has experimented with Carnatic music system by keeping its rich tradition untouched. Ragas like Ganapathi, Sarvashri, Mahati, Lavangi, etc., are credited to him. Balamuralikrishna has over four hundred compositions to his credit and is one of the very few people to have composed in all of the seventy-two melakarta ragas. Additionally, created several ragas, with four notes and three notes, and invented a new tala system. His compositions encompass every facet in Carnatic music that include varnas, krithis, tillanas and bhavageethas.

Epilogue

I hope you enjoyed this musical journey! The richness of Indian classical music has to be experienced in order to be fully comprehended. I urge you to listen to Indian classical music with an open mind, particularly to the great maestros of the past, who have transcended technique and grammar, taking the listeners into the realm of pure emotion. In music, as in the other performing arts, doing is learning. Take the various concepts in this book and apply them—play with them, try out new things, listen to how musicians bring music out in practice, and see how you can use it in your preferred musical genre. For instance, when you read about the concept of nadai, you will get an idea of what it means to divide a beat into three equal parts or five equal parts. But if you listen to a practical application of that, for instance the Mohana varnam that I've played in fifteen speeds (with the legendary mridangam genius Palghat Mani Iyer), you will get a better idea of what it means. And when you try to sing a tisra nadai pattern or play a khanda nadai pattern on your instrument, you will get a much clearer picture.

Music naturally teaches us to be more creative. An Indian classical musician may take a raga with just five notes and sing or play an instrument for an hour using various permutations and combinations. Starting with a little motif and then expanding it into a musical phrase and large sentences by varying the dynamics and adding ornamentations, a musician can create strong emotions and give life to the improvisation. This calls for a lot of imagination and creativity, which can be applied easily to other fields as well. The presence of mind that a musician learns helps in dealing with various situations outside of music as well.

Indian classical music, particularly in south India, has a strong spiritual base. The emotions of devotion or surrender are prevalent in many compositions of Indian music. We consider music as one of the ways to realise the ultimate truth. It is important to recognise this sacred aspect of music in order to offer ourselves to it with dedication and sincerity. It is only then that we realise that music can take us beyond boundaries.

I gained everything because of music and it is an inseparable part of my life. I hope music becomes a part of your life too...